I0011145

50 Tips for Simple and Safe Searching

(English\Spanish)

Jan 2015

From the Tech Simple and Easy Series

Thomas Lahey

DEDICATION

To anyone and everyone trying to make life a bit easier for the rest of us.

Copyright © 2014 Thomas Lahey

All rights reserved.

CONTENTS

CONTENIDO

The book is separated into two parts; the first is in English the second part is in Spanish. My thanks to Janet Reeves who translated these tips into Spanish.

INTRODUCTION

To keep it short and simple I am going to focus on the most popular search provider which of course is Google. I am also going to focus on the Chrome and Internet Explorer (IE) browsers. Although I believe there are strong reasons to only use Chrome or IE, the same is not true for searching. If you really like Bing or Yahoo for search that's fine. Many of the tips apply even if you are using these providers.

Microsoft Bing support pages;
- http://onlinehelp.microsoft.com/en-us/bing
- http://onlinehelp.microsoft.com/en-us/bing/ff808438.aspx

Yahoo Search support pages;
- https://help.yahoo.com/kb/search

I have used Google for many years and know my fair share of tricks and tips. However, like too much today everything changes often, making it hard to keep up. This also makes it hard to find documentation that's up-to-date. Everyone's goal is naturally intuitive applications with little need for documentation. So perhaps one day tips, tricks, and cheat sheets will be a thing of the past. We can only hope.

Here's my take on Google search tips for Jan 2015 after I revisited my somewhat outdated tips. The sad fact is a few years back there were a lot more great references on Google search. There were even Google posters for the classroom. Perhaps now it's assumed that everyone knows search and it's so intuitive that there's not a big need for reference materials. Search itself is evolving and there are some elements that are moving to apps (see my What's New in 2015 section). However, there are still some great tips not everyone knows and you should find some here.

As things change often, I am sure within a few months at least one set of steps will be out of date because of a change. Hopefully the change will be minor and it will be easy for you to find the new steps. The pace of change especially in browsers is in the twilight zone.

Having automatic updates is very good for security. However, you may realize that some of the menus or settings are different than you remember. You're not going crazy, it's the tech world's constant updates not you.

I had to add a few tips to make sure your search experience is working as expected. The first few tips are to make sure Chrome and IE are working properly and not using some evil add-on or toolbar (I know not all toolbars are evil). You also can't think about search without thinking about safety, so I have some tips there as well.

NEW FOR 2015

A big change is coming in search and you may not know it's on the horizon. Years ago everyone went to Google.com and searched. Now most people know that you can just type into the URL bar at the top of your browser and search. This made it easier for everyone. You can still go to Google.com and search and use advanced options (covered later).

What's new are voice assistants, Siri, Google Now, and Cortana. Initially they were used mainly for voice search. However, they now allow commands like wake-me-up to tell your phone to set your alarm. These have their own syntax (format and key words). But they are entered in the search bar or with the mic option.

I don't think there is much overlap or confusion now but I can see where some people might get confused. If you type or speak "wake me up" into the search bar looking for song lyrics from Evanescence, don't be surprised if your phone wants to set your alarm instead.

If all the key commands for search started with the word "Search" it would be easier but that's not the case. So in the near future you will have to know some of these formats to avoid any confusion. I have a few Google Now tips and links at the end of this book.

This falls into "I have to keep somewhat current on technology or I won't understand how to use it anymore". Hopefully all the great new things we can do with technology will help offset the pain of constantly staying up-to-date on how to use it.

Let's start with some key points and a recap of the best tips. This is sort of a condensed version of the best of these tips.

Some key points;
- Tips relating to security and safety will change over time but they never get less important.
- As search gets better and better some of these tips are less useful (Quotes, Exclude, Wildcards), but that's a good thing.
- Search and voice assistants such as Siri and Google Now are merging and that impacts how you will search and use your devices.
- Chrome is the only browser on all major platforms (Win, Mac, Android, iPhone), and it's very good. So it's what you should be using. Internet Explorer (IE) wins on child safety features, but it requires understanding of windows accounts.
- If you haven't heard of two-step verification you should look it up.
- If you're a student and haven't used Google scholar give it a spin, especially the Cite link below each result.
- Consider buying a Chromebook, they are all most people need and make life **much easier**. They have a few limitations but they are very affordable. Some people tell me not having Skype is why they won't buy one; however, Google Hangouts is a great replacement for Skype, and Skype may be coming.

For those of you who just want to get directly to the point (hey, everyone's impatient) and want the 10 most awesome tips, here they are. Let me know if you agree on the 10.

Top Awesome Tips
- # 1 Start with a little fun, cool search tips and games.
- # 2 Stay Safe, use current browser versions, anti-virus.
- # 7 Use Chrome as your browser.
- # 9 Use two-step verification.
- #23 Use Google advance search.
- #31 Search for Movie times in Google, clean no movie adds.
- #36 Use Google Scholar for research and easy citations.

- #40 Use Google custom search, create your own search.
- #43 Search and browse anonymously.
- #50 Google Now commands, voice search and commands.

For anyone else, and even for those impatient readers from above, here is the full list.

Tip #1
Start with a little fun.

There is a little more fun in tech things these days, perhaps trying to offset the stuff that drives us crazy. So here are a few tips and tricks in Google search. A number of the fun tips like this don't work anymore because Google changed its use of automatic results. Everything seems to be constantly changing, it's hard to keep track.

- In Google search **tilt**.
- In Google search **do a barrel roll**.
- In Google search (sqrt(cos(x))*cos(400*x)+sqrt (abs(x))-0.4)*(4-x*x)^0.1 (who says mathematicians don't have feelings).
- There are many more, search for **fun google tips**.
- You can go to Google Doodles (www.google.com/doodles).

Tip #2
Stay safe and keep up to date.

I wish things were a bit simpler for online safety; however, there continue to be major efforts in safety. I cover a number of tips on these issues here. Here is a short recap and some key links;

For children's online access (specific tips to follow);
- Never allow small children unsupervised access to the internet.
- IE (10 or higher is best) with family filter on.
- Use Google as your search provider.

- Turn on Google SafeSearch.
- Make sure your computer is up-to-date.
- Make sure your browser is up-to-date.
- Have an up-to-date antivirus program installed.
- Don't assume public places such as libraries are 100% safe.

Some links on safety:
- https://kids.usa.gov/online-safety/index.shtml
- https://www.onguardonline.gov/articles/0006-talk-your-kids
- http://www.nationalcac.org/prevention/internet-safety-kids.html

There are a number of tips that follow that cover many of these items. To stay up-to-date, bookmark the links above and check to see what's new from time to time.

Tip #3
For small children, <u>only use</u> Google search.

Here are a few places where online filtering occurs:
- Network level, for schools, libraries, companies.
- System level, computer or tablet's operating system (OS).
- Software filters antivirus, etc.
- Browsers (IE, Chrome, Firefox, etc.) depending on their settings.
- Search provider used, Google, Bing, and Yahoo.

For search, Google, Bing, and Yahoo have key differences. The main difference is that Google generally filters out a great deal of adult content automatically. For all its great and grand powers of search, Goggle has decided adult content will not be one of them.

Don't assume you can't find adult content using Google search (you can), but the chances of adult content especially pictures, accidently showing up are much lower on Google. Everyone makes typing errors and we don't want any surprises.

To set Google as your search provider for Chrome:
1. Select **Menu > Settings > Search**.
2. Choose **Google** from the drop-down menu.

To set Google as your search provider for most versions of IE:
1. Select **Tools > Manager Add-ons >Search Providers**.
2. Highlight **Google**.
3. Select **Set as Default** (bottom right).
4. Select **Close**.

It's a lot harder than you think to make sure you are actually using Google search. Browser hijacks are fairly common and people often search in the URL area and don't go to Google.com. Please read tips on resetting your browser and you should be good.

Tip #4
Use Google SafeSearch.

Google has its own safety settings for search. Regardless of which browser you are using it will work. You can and should use it in addition to other safety features.

It's very easy to set and also allows you to lock it with your account.

To turn on Google SafeSearch in your browser:
1. Go to http://www.google.com/preferences.
2. Check the box **Filter explicit results**.
3. You can lock SafeSearch, but it requires you log in to a Google account for it to work.

Information on SafeSearch:
https://support.google.com/websearch/answer/510?hl=en

Tip #5
For small children, consider using Internet Explorer.

I love Chrome, but for all its advantages, it still lacks some basic safety filters. I am sure Chrome will have enhanced filters soon but today it falls behind Internet Explorer (IE). If a small child is running a Google search or is online at all, you should consider using Internet Explorer (IE) version 10 or higher. Of course no small child should have unsupervised access to the Internet. Schools and public libraries generally have good search filters in place, but nothing is 100%.

IE versions get somewhat complicated, so in some cases you may not be able to upgrade to IE 10 or 11 but many earlier versions also support the Family Safety feature.

To set IE safe settings for most versions:
1. **Tools**.
2. **Internet Options**.
3. **Content**.
4. **Family Safety**.

You may get prompted for setting up a new user account, or be told your account is an Administrative account when you go to Family Safety. If this is the case and you don't fully understand how to setup accounts and Windows permissions, you should find someone to help or skip it. I don't want you locked out of windows.

Microsoft information for online safety:
- http://windows.microsoft.com/en-US/windows-8/family-safety
- http://www.microsoft.com/security/family-safety/childsafety-age.aspx

Tip #6
Computers shared by children should be setup appropriately.

Many computers are shared by several people. A simple tip to help would be for children to use IE (with the Family Safety Feature on). Everyone else can use Chrome or another browser that is hidden (not on the Start menu or tabs, etc.)

- Any computer used by a child should have all the safety features on.
- Another method to help is to "not" provide the computer password to children. This makes sure you know when they are online.

Tip #7
Use Chrome as a browser (mostly).

Yes, this comes right after a tip that says use IE for young children. Like most things in life, one solution does not work for everything. Overall, Chrome is the best browser and I strongly recommend it with the one exception for small children. Once they're teenagers, assume they will be able to find a way around any filters or limits. It's an easy search to find out how to bypass these filters, steal a car etc. Yes it's a brave new world, and the challenges are bigger than ever.

So, to make life simpler just use Chrome.

Since Apple gave up on Windows browsers, it's not even a two horse race. There is only one major player who has a browser on all platforms and that's Google's Chrome. Microsoft will most probably never have a full version of IE for the iPhone, and IE on Android. Remote IE is a poor work-around.

Chrome should work on 99% of websites regardless of your device (phone, tablet, or computer). It also has some great features that work with Google search and Google apps. There are still some minor differences between Chrome for different platforms (Windows, Mac, and Android).

Tip #8
Sign in to Google to use Chrome.

If your computer, phone, or tablet is only going to be used by you it's easy, just sign into your Google account.

To sign in to Google:
1. **Menu**.
2. **Settings**
3. **Sign in**
4. Enter your account

Signing in gives you a number of benefits, such as synchronizing Chrome across all your devices. Items such as your bookmarks work on the computer, phone, and tablet. Chrome supports multiple users, which gets somewhat confusing, so keep that in mind. When you sign in, Google remembers your searches and this in turn helps your future searches. Some people like this, some don't. If you want to search anonymously, there's a simple solution in an upcoming tip.

If multiple people who have their own Google accounts use the same computer, each person can sign in with their own account. This is somewhat confusing. People tend to forget and use the computer when logged into the wrong account. It might be better to not sign in with Chrome on a shared computer.

Tip #9
Use two-step verification to sign in.

This is not directly related to search, but if you're logging into a Google or Apple account you should be using this. What it means is you need more than a password to log in. You need a code from your phone or other device as well. The code changes every time. This makes it much harder (just about impossible) for anyone to hack into your account.
There are some key differences in how two-step verification works with Apple and Google and the process can be a little confusing. I

am not going to cover all the steps here but will provide some links that should help.

- For Apple two-step your phone gets a confirmation code when you want to login. You need this code to login. You can also set it to remember your device.
- For Google, after the first time you enter a code on your device, you can tell Google to remember this device, computer, or tablet and it won't require a code again. Any time a new device tries to access your account Google will require at least a first time code to sign in.
- For Google it uses cookies to remember that you don't want to be prompted for the code again on this device. So if you clear your cookies, you will get the code requirement again.
- Also, if you use two-step and have Google Hangouts as your default message app on your phone, it's potentially a problem. Your Hangout account could be locked waiting for a password, but you can only get it from Hangouts. I had a fun time with this once.
- Google is already moving beyond two-step to more of an integrated system between all your devices that is secure but does not always need the two-step code.
- Google also has backup codes for two-step which are fantastic!

Some key links on Two-Step
- http://www.google.com/landing/2step/
- http://support.apple.com/kb/ht5570

With recent account hacks of famous actresses Apple is trying to make some needed updates to security, and they continue to improve all the time.

Tip #10
Make sure Chrome or Internet Explorer is up-to-date.

For current versions of Chrome this is not a problem as Chrome automatically updates. If for some reason you have an older version that is not updated, it's easy to fix. First, if you see the Chrome menu (three bars at the top right) green, orange, or red it means Chrome is out of date. If you see a wrench in the top right corner, not the three bars, your using a fairly old version (they changed the wrench to three bars in 2012). When the menu is highlighted in color then **Update Google Chrome** should show up under the menu. You may have to restart Chrome after the update.

Chrome updates;
1. Menu (three bars at the top right), also called hotdog.
2. **About Google Chrome**.
3. **Google Chrome is up to date** should be checked, if not select **Update Google Chrome**. In most cases a Chrome restart is not required.

For current versions of Internet Explorer (IE) this is also not a problem, IE automatically updates. You should have Windows updates set to automatic as well so that all the updates and safety features are automatically installed.

To install updates for most IE versions:
1. **Help**.
2. **About Internet Explorer**.
3. **Install new versions automatically** (should be checked).

Tip #11
Reset Chrome or IE to default settings.

Yes, even Chrome is not impervious to browser hacks. It took Google "way too long" but Chrome now has a reset feature. This is not an option for Chrome for phones as there are not currently many features, so you are relatively safe from hackers (for now). If your computer's browser has already been hacked, often it's the search area that's impacted, and you will need a reset.

In any case, a reset for Chrome is a good idea.

This reset clears everything except saved passwords, bookmarks and custom search engine's (hot tips on this coming up). If you use any extensions, it will only turn them off, not removed them, so you can turn them back on.

To reset Chrome (Windows, Mac):
1. Chrome menu (three bars top right), also called hotdog.
2. **Settings** (go to the bottom).
3. **Show Advanced Settings** (again go to the very bottom).
4. **Reset Settings**.

You might notice Chrome runs faster (this is a happy thing).

Chrome reset information:
https://support.google.com/chrome/answer/3296214?p=ui_reset_settings&rd=1

Resetting IE gets a little more complicated as it **resets the safety and security settings.** So you will have to reconfigure these settings if you do a reset. **If you already have the family safety features on, I would not reset IE**. If all of this is new to you, reset IE, and then add in the family safety features.

To reset IE (most versions)
1. **Tools**.
2. **Internet Options**.
3. **Advanced** tab.
4. **Reset**.
5. **Tools**.
6. **Internet**.
7. **Options**.
8. **Content**.
9. **Family Safety**.

Again, you may get prompted for setting up a new user account, or be told your account is an Administrative account when you go to Family Safety. If this is the case and you don't fully understand how to setup accounts and Windows permissions, you should ask for help or skip it. It's a good feature, but I don't want anyone locked out of

Windows. I would love Microsoft to have an option to just put a password on the Family Safety feature.

Microsoft IE reset information: support.microsoft.com/kb/923737

Tip #12
Make Google your default search engine.

For Chrome on Windows computers or Macs if you already followed the prior tip you are good. If for some reason you didn't reset Chrome or want to make sure it's correct on your phone or tablet, here are the steps.

To set Google as the default search engine for Chrome on Windows:
1. Menu - top right three bars (also known as hot dog).
2. **Settings**.
3. **Search**.
4. **Manage Search Engines**.
5. Choose Google as Default.
6. **Done**.

To set Google as the default search engine for Chrome on a Mac:
1. Menu - top right three bars (hot dog).
2. **Settings**.
3. **Search**.
4. **Manage Search Engines**.
5. Choose Google as Default.
6. **Done**.

To set Google as the default search engine for an iPhone:
1. Menu - top right three bars (hot dog).
2. **Settings**.
3. **Search Engine**.
4. **Google**.
5. **Done**.

To set Google as the default search engine for an Android phone:
1. Use the menu button on the bottom.

2. **Settings**.
3. **Search engine**
4. Select Google.

To set Google as the default search engine for IE (most versions):
1. **Tools**.
2. **Manage Add-ons**.
3. **Search Providers**.
4. Highlight Google.
5. **Set as Default** if it's not already (Bottom right).
6. **Close**.

Tip #13
Use an antivirus program.

This is sadly confusing for Windows. This is because when you buy a computer it already has an antivirus product installed that will soon expire (sometimes in 60 to 90 days). You should only have one antivirus product running on your computer so they have turned off Microsoft's own free program. They were paid by the antivirus company to do this and it's not a great situation.

Apple computers have built-in antivirus software working by default and it's free and great. If you want to buy something else there are a number of options. Chromebooks don't need antivirus software and hopefully it will stay that way, which is one of many reasons to buy one.

Most Windows antivirus programs have a subscription model. You have to pay **every year** or it will stop working which is not great.

The other choice is to figure out how to remove the program that came with your Windows computer and install something else with several free choices including Microsoft's own antivirus software (Security Essentials for Windows 7 and Windows Defender for Windows 8). **If you are lucky you know someone who can help.**

For Windows 8 (and the upcoming Windows 10), the good news is you don't have to install Windows defender. It's automatically there **and can't be removed**. However, it can be disabled and this is done if another antivirus software program is installed. Again, you should not have more than one enabled at the same time.

I have mixed feelings on what to recommend for Windows due to these issues. Microsoft's free antivirus software usually does not rank at the top for protection, but it's free and will automatically update itself. It won't stop working because you have not paid for another year etc.

So, my suggestion if you don't know someone who can help and are not that great with computers, is to **carefully** buy the license for the antivirus that came with your computer.

If you are spending $1,400 on a system and money is not really an issue buy the deluxe antivirus package etc. If you are buying a $300 computer and $200 extra for a deluxe antivirus program is more than you can afford, only buy the basic antivirus ($20-$40). Another option is to buy a Chromebook, which does everything most people need for a fantastic price. It does not need an antivirus program. I don't want to suggest any "Best" store, but there is one and it is generally the best place to get advice when you are buying a computer. They will of course want to sell you the most expensive anti-virus program.

Chromebook Information:
http://www.google.com/intl/en/chrome/devices/features/

Tip #14
Use Google's search support pages.

Google has its own pages on search and they have some great tips. Just know that Google like everyone else has lots of reference materials (which change often). Occasionally some tips are slightly out of date, but it should be 98%.

Spend a few minutes on these pages and you should be able to rock Search. Because there are Google Search, Patent Search, Scholar, Google Now, and more, not everything is in the following links. I cover these specialized searches in my tips and included links within the tips, so keep reading.

Google search support:
- http://www.google.com/insidesearch/
- http://www.google.com/insidesearch/tipstricks/
- http://www.google.com/insidesearch/tipstricks/all.html
- http://www.google.com/insidesearch/searcheducation/index.html

Tip #15
Search directly in your browser's URL bar.

In case you missed it, the easiest way to search is to just type in the URL bar at the top of your browser. This works with all browsers. If you seem to get a lot of ads or other junk in your results, go to www.google.com and search from there. If you get different results, your browser or computer may have been hacked.

If these results are different you can reset your browser per the prior tips to see if that resolves the issue.

Tip #16
Enlarge your search results to make them easier to read.

Using the browser to search is much better if you can read what you're looking for. You can change the screen resolution so you can see your screen better. This process is basically the same across browsers and platforms. Here are some common methods to change the resolution.

To change the screen resolution for Chrome for Windows:

- Use the **Ctrl** key, for bigger (**Ctrl+**), smaller (**Ctrl-**), and reset (**Ctrl0**).
- For a mouse with a wheel, press **Ctrl** and roll up or down.
- Menu (3 bars) **Zoom** (use + and – to change).
- **F11** goes to full screen; just don't forget F11 takes you back to normal.

To change the screen resolution for IE for Windows (most versions)
- The **Ctrl** key, for bigger (**Ctrl+**), smaller (**Ctrl-**), and reset (**Ctrl0**).
- For a mouse with a wheel, press **Ctrl** and roll up or down
- Menu (3 bars) **Zoom** (use + and – to change)
- F11 goes to full screen; just don't forget F11 takes you back to normal.

To change the screen resolution for Chrome for a Mac:
- The Mac Command key (⌘), for bigger (⌘ +), smaller (⌘ -).
- Mouse wheel scrolling does not work on a Mac.
- Menu - top right three bars (also known as hot dog).
- **Zoom** (use + and – to change).

Tip #17
"How" and "Where" you search from matters.

There is a lot of effort on voice search and Google Now. Not everyone is used to speaking into a computer or phone but it's the future. Google interprets these items differently just as it interprets things differently if you are logged into your account or have history on your computer or browser. Where you search from impacts your results (usually just slightly).

For good or bad Google wants to know about you so it can better help you and increase its ad revenue.

Many of the following tips apply to both typed search, voice search and Google Now. If you search on a different computer it may have different settings and the results can be somewhat different. Again Google does a great job finding your results; just don't be surprised if they are a little different depending on where you search.

Also, if your browser has content or family filters on, your results may be different.

Tip #18
"When" you search matters.

Things can change very frequently and Google assumes you are searching for current information (hot topics). For most searches this works in your favor. If your trying to search something a bit back in time you may need to add more information in your search including years or dates. More on this later.

Searching for product prices including air fares and more costly items is more complicated. Most companies who sell online, use complex algorithms to set prices and they can change hourly. Sort of like some theaters selling discount movie tickets on Tuesday nights because they know it's a slow night.

So you're not going crazy, prices can change often.

Tip #19
Start simple and add words as needed.

You should always start simple with just a few words. Once you see the results you'll get a much better idea on what to add or subtract (yes you can do that). Long questions sometimes give you unexpected results so start short and then add words for better results.

Search steps:

- Start simple with just a few words.
- Review results.
- Add, subtract or exclude words (Tip 22) for better results.
- Repeat as needed.

Tip #20
You probably don't need to use quotes.

Google does a great job of searching for all the words you list; however, it's not looking at your "exact" words or phrase. Putting items in quotes will look for a direct match. You can also use wildcards (*) within the quotes, but if you put them in the wrong place you could get worse results Use wildcards only if you have a clear idea of where to put them.

This is becoming less important as Google is getting scary good at interpreting what you are asking for.

Quote tips from Google:
https://support.google.com/websearch/answer/136861?hl=en

Tip #21
Use an * (asterisk) for wildcard searches.

You can use the * (asterisk) as a wildcard when searching. This works best if you have the search in quotes. Again Google search is getting so good that this tip is less useful then it used to be.

However, if you combine quotes, wildcards and exclude with the – (next tip), you'll have a powerful combination.

Wildcard example directly from Google:
" a * saved is a * earned"

Tip #22
Exclude a word from a search.

Yes you can do that; you simply use the minus sign. Sometimes a word is associated with more than one item and you want to remove it.

Exclude example directly from Google:
jaguar –car

This is when you are looking for the animal not the car. Of course that does not block auto or other words for cars. This goes back to the tip to start simple. If you find some results you don't want and they have a common word you can exclude it.

Exclude tips from Google (yes it's on the same page):
https://support.google.com/websearch/answer/136861?hl=en

Tip #23
Use Google advanced search.

There are lots of tips, shortcuts etc. for search. Some people love these shortcuts and have them memorized. However, you don't have to remember them, just go to advanced search. Advanced search can usually be found by clicking on Settings (bottom right of Google main page).

If you don't see Settings on the bottom of the main Google page, run a search (on anything) and then click on the options gear (top right) and choose Advanced Search.

Advance Search key choices:
- All.
- Exact phrase.
- None (words to exclude).

- Last Update.
- Safe Search.
- Usage rights.

Advanced Search web page:
http://www.google.com/advanced_search

Advanced search help:
https://support.google.com/websearch/answer/35890?hl=en

Tip #24
Your search results include search tools, also called tabs.

This gets a little complicated (OK, a lot complicated) and Google could do a better job at this, so it will take a little explaining. I give Google a C- for this.

When you search for something it generally defaults to a **Web Search**, and you can refine the search using quotes, wildcards, the minus sign, etc.

In your search results, you might get something like this at the top of the page.

Web Shopping Images Videos Maps More Search Tools

However, due to algorithms, rules and Google trying its best to provide you with the best possible results; the list, order and search tools topics change. So you could get something like this.

Web **Images** News Videos Shopping More Search Tools

Depending on what Google thinks you're looking for, it presents you with appropriate choices to narrow down the results. Most of these choices make sense, some don't. Generally Google does a fantastic job of finding what you want (we all know that). But, it doesn't always give you clear and consistent choices to filter these results. An example of this is the Hotels tab. You may not see a tab for this, but if you choose Flights, it becomes a choice.

I am not going through all the options here but most choices have a **Time Filter** which is probably the most useful. Also some results have a sorting option such as

- Sorted by relevance.
- Sorted by date.

Sorted by relevance (which is the default) usually works best.

The best advice I can give is to look at the choices and see what gets you closer to what you want. Some of the best filters including time are under

- **Search Tools** (which has some great choices).

Tip #25
Search for a specific document type (filetype).

If you're looking for documents not web pages, and you know the document type, you can search specifically for that file type. An example would be filetype:pdf World War 1 where the extension comes after filetype:. So in this example the search is looking for PDF documents about World War I.

This is often useful if you are looking for data sets that you can use in analysis or graphs.

filetype sample searches:

- filetype:pdf World War 1.
- filetype:doc World War 1.

filetypes that Google commonly indexes:
https://support.google.com/webmasters/answer/35287?hl=en

Tip #26
Use search to convert almost anything.

Google will convert almost anything. Type what you want to convert and you should get an answer. Just be sure you know what you're asking. You can't convert pints to pounds. In the US, pints are a measure of volume and pounds are a measure of weight. Five pints of water will weigh less than five pints of lead.

However, as long as the measures are the same, such as distance (miles to km), etc. it will work. You can also phrase these as a question "How many inches in 37 miles?" and you will get an answer. That's the amazing power of search today; you can input almost anything and get an answer.

You can also convert some scientific measures such as temperature, energy, force, electric current, etc. Some great webpages and apps do a better job for more complex problems. However, Google is free and simple and you can start there.

Conversion examples:
- 5 miles to km (will give you 8.04672).
- 5 USD to Yen
- 2344320 inches to mile (will give you 37 miles).

Conversion and math tips:
https://support.google.com/websearch/answer/3284611?hl=en

Tip #27
Use search to do math.

Google can do an amazing amount of math if you just input the formula. One of the fun tips in the beginning was to use math to create a heart shape.

When you enter a formula in search, Google will present the answer with its online calculator. It does a good job and includes many features.

However, like the conversion tip above there are many outstanding math apps for phones and tablets these days. I imagine many people will be using these. There's a big visual difference between web page results and a phone app. The app is easier to use and easier to read. Another feature\tip that is fading, but its being replace by something better.

Math functions available:
- Basic math.
- Functions such as sin, cos, tan.
- Plotting including 3D graphs (depending on your browser).

Conversion and math tips (same as above):
https://support.google.com/websearch/answer/3284611?hl=en

Tip #28
Search for public data sets and graph the results.

Google has a good number of public data sets that can be searched and accessed. You can find this information on your own from the source, but it may not be as easy to search and use. It's also convenient to have so many data sets all in one location.

Google has a nice data explorer graphing tool that lets you visualize the data. You can also share your graph with a link. Unfortunately at this time Google does not allow you to export the data, only a link to the source, which should allow some method of download.

Some of the data sets are fairly outdated (two or three years old), so you might want to review the dates for your data set before you begin.

Public data features:
- https://www.google.com/publicdata/directory
- Large sets of data from many sources.
- Nice graphing feature.
- Ability to create chart and create link to it.
- No data export.

Tip #29
Search for flight Status.

Google purchased a flight software company (ITA) a few years back, so they have direct access to flight information. They can't sell tickets because people use Google to search for ticket prices and Google would have an unfair advantage.

Flight search example (carrier and the flight number):
- Southwest 234

Flight information from Google (across most carriers):
- https://www.google.com/flights

Flightstats has some good tracking as well (not a Google product):
- http://www.flightstats.com/go/Home/home.do

Tip #30
Find the delivery status for a shipped package (UPS, USPS, FedEx, etc.)

Google has real time package tracking (UPS, USPS, FedEx). All you need to do is enter the package number in search and it will bring up the tracking information. UPS, FedEx, and others have more than one number format. Usually putting in the tracking number by itself works. However, if you have issues you can add the prefix such as FedEx then the number (FedEx is normally 12 or 15 digits) to get better results.

Package Search Samples;
- 345676545675 or.
- FedEx 345676545675.

Tip #31
Search for movie times.

I love Fandango and related websites and apps that show trailers and movie times. However sometimes I just get tired of the previews and ads that pop up and "just want to see the movie times." Just search with the word **movies** and you should see a list of local movies. Click on the movie and you will get local movie times.

Fandango seems to have a slight edge in accuracy. On rare occasions I have seen Google movie times behind a day. Movie theaters shift movies and times to match demand often. Fandango sells tickets and has more direct access to theater times.

Perhaps some smart Google employee can write a little script to compare their movie times against the others to flag and resolve discrepancies.

To search for movie times:
- Search for the word **movie**.
- Click on the movie to get show times.

Movie times by theater (simple and awesome):
http://www.google.com/movies

Searching can find amazing things, time travel exists, movies for $1:
http://www.starplexcinemas.com/locations.php?theaterid=3002

Tip #32
Find weather forecasts.

These days there are more places and apps to find a weather forecast than you can count. Google has its own, which is simple and clean. If you don't want too much info and "just want a simple forecast" it's a good place to go.

To search for the weather forecast:
- Type **forecast** followed by the city and state or use the ZIP code.
- Forecast Concord, CA.
- Forecast 94521.

US National Weather Service as an alternate:
http://www.weather.gov/

Tip #33
Search for stock prices.

You can search for stock prices by just putting in the stock symbol. There are many apps including Google's own Finance that let you track your stocks, but it you just want a quick view this will get the job done.

To search for a stock price:

- Enter the stock symbol in search and you will get stock price, an example would be csco for Cisco
- If the stock symbol is the same as the company name such as IBM, you will get links on the left but the stock price will be on the right. Click on the stock price and then you will get the

chart.

Stock market info from Google:
https://www.google.com/finance

Stock market sites from other sources (Google isn't best at everything):
- http://finance.yahoo.com/market-overview/
- http://markets.wsj.com/usoverview?mod=WSJ_hpp_marketdata
- http://www.bloomberg.com/markets/
- http://investing.money.msn.com/investments/market-summary/

Tip #34
Search for a location by city or ZIP code.

You can search locally by adding the city name or zip after your search. Although most people are moving to search within map applications, it's a bit easier and you can see the locations. Again people are moving to Google Now with cards and the trend will only increase. A Google card is a short summary of useful information, usually based on the time of day and your location. Think of traffic, appointments, weather or a sports team scores.

Also, Google usually knows your location by default if you are logged in, so this tip is best used for other locations. Say you are planning a trip and want to search your destination for the best pizza in New York, etc.

Location search samples:
- Pizza New York
- Pizza 10001.

Tip #35
Use Google Patent Search.

Google has a great patent reference that is both fun and educational.

It's a great resource for everyone. I think you will find it much easier to use then the government site, which I have also included below.

Google Patent Search:
  https://www.google.com/?tbm=pts&gws_rd=ssl

Google Advanced Patent Search:
  http://www.google.com/advanced_patent_search

Google Patent Search – About:
  https://support.google.com/faqs/answer/2539193?hl=en&ref_topic=3368954

US government Patent Search site for reference:
  http://www.uspto.gov/patents/process/search/index.jsp

Tip #36
Set up a Google Scholar student profile.

Google has a search specifically for students; it has lots of great features including Patent Search (tip #9) built in. What makes this so fantastic are the many awesome features. I would suggest setting up a scholar profile to save your references.

Profiles take just a minute to setup:
  http://scholar.google.com/intl/en/scholar/citations.html.

Google Scholar key features:
- Great searches including patents and case law.
- Can save your searches\articles.
- Gives the properly formatted citation (all three major formats).
- Properly formatted citations (**Repeated & Awesome**).
- Cited by numbers and related articles.
- Library Links, lets you link to subscriptions in your school\library. It's a bit technical, but a home run for college students. The library and or school tech department should

be able to help.

Google Scholar Search:
http://scholar.google.com/

Google Scholar Search Tips:
http://scholar.google.com/intl/en-US/scholar/help.html

An example of searching in Google Scholar with Cite

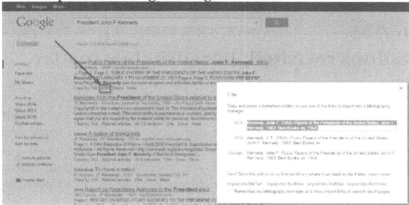

Tip #37
Use the Google Docs research tool.

There is an awesome way to put research information into a Google document and automatically add a proper citation. Once you search for something and put in into a document you are covered and your teacher should be happy. It's not as comprehensive as Google Scholar, but has many of the same features. It does make it easier to put the data into a Google document.

What is does is create a side pane on the right with you search and results. There are a number of key features that make creating a paper very easy.

Google Docs research benefits:
- Creates a side panel for easy viewing.

- Works with Google docs, not spreadsheets or slides.
- Hover over the links first for Preview, Insert Link, or Cite.
- If you cite the research, Google will automatically add it to your document.

Google Docs Research help
- https://support.google.com/docs/answer/2481802?hl=en

Tip #38
Citations revisited, because they matter.

Sometimes I just want to add a related tip. Because online citations are such an issue I am going to provide some additional resources for them. Most kids should already be using one or more of these and some are easier to use. A school or teacher may prefer one or another. What they always need are correctly formatted online citations. My kids used easybib, which seems to be the most popular, but there are others out there.

If you're a parent and you are not familiar with them, take a minute to review at least one. There should be no reason your child gets marked off a paper for an improper citation.

Citation resources alternatives:
- http://www.easybib.com/
- http://www.mendeley.com/
- http://www.bibme.org/

Tip #39
Find and read public domain books for free.

Google has a specific search just for books, with many you can preview or read for free. You can link your Google profile with

Google books for a personal library. Google is still a ways away from a truly unified account, so these links and setup are required.

I am also going to list a link to project Gutenberg which is another great book reference. Nothing to do with Google however it's also a great reference.

Google Book Search:
http://books.google.com/

Google Book Help:
https://support.google.com/books/?hl=en#topic=4359341

Project Gutenberg Search:
http://www.gutenberg.org/

Tip #40
Use Google custom search.

<u>**Yes, it's both amazing and awesome**</u>. This is one of the most underutilized features around. There are a number of people who use this and it is most commonly used by teachers. There are just a great deal of uses for this.

Not only can you take the power of Google search and customize it, you can share it with the world, post it on you web page and more.

To use Google custom search (you need to be logged in):
1. https://www.google.com/cse/all.
2. Click **New Search Engine** (top left).
3. Add pages and or sites that you want to include.
4. Give it a name (whatever you want to call it).
5. Click **Create** (at the bottom).

Now you can add it to your website, or make it a public URL that you can share or have other people link to.

Google custom search information:

https://support.google.com/customsearch/?hl=en#topic=4513742

There are a number of schools and teachers who use this but I just can't imagine why it's not being used "everywhere." So if you are teaching history and have a great list of 30 reference sites on American history and you want to make it available for your students, it's a 10 minute task to get it done.

If you're a fossils fan and love everything about them, you even run your own group at the local museum on Thursday nights. You can set up your own search that covers the best 20 websites that cover this topic.

If you are a school administer for an elementary school or you're a parent who is homeschooling your kids and want them to have a really safe search you could do this. Just note, I think you could cover a lot of information with 30-40 websites. This is great for smaller kids, but this won't work for older kids who would need a very broad search area.

If anyone wants to compile 1,500 great sites for education that would cover 95% of what any student would need, that would be great. We could just have our kids search that without fear of something inappropriate showing up. Hey I think you could do a great job with just 500 sites.

Tip #41
Use Google Alerts.

Searching is good, but what if there was an easy way to have Google send you what you are looking for? At one time there was Google Reader which was a RSS reader. RSS readers still exist, but they are not as popular as some people thought they would be.

Google still has Google Alerts, which is a Google search that will automatically email you when a new item shows up. Let's say your company works on lithium batteries and you try to keep up on the latest news. You could still search, but you could also tell Google to send you an alert every time.

To set up Google Alerts:
1. Go to this webpage:
2. https://www.google.com/alerts?hl=en&tab=33.
3. Type in a word or phrase.
4. Click **Create Alert** (the default options usually work best).
5. If you're not already signed in, it will prompt you to sign in.
6. Your email account will start to receive daily alerts (that's the default).

Additional information:
- You can set up as many alerts as you wish. Some people create a separate Gmail account just to get the alerts and just review it at the start of the week.
- One major advantage of alerts is you know by date when they first show up and any related follow-up.

Google Alerts information:
https://support.google.com/alerts/?hl=en

Tip #42
Reserved, as it's the answer for everything.

If you are interested look it up. It was also the first building number in the giant Googleplex.

Tip #43
Search and browse anonymously (it's complicated and therefore a long tip, sorry).

You can delete history for both search and browsing. You can also turn off history in almost all cases, so it's always off. Chrome has no easy way to turn off history and I hope one day they will change it. Please remember I am only going to cover Google search and your browser history. I am not going to cover all the places that are tracking you, but here are some.

You are being tracked by:
- Your search provider (Google, Bing, Yahoo).
- Your browser.
- Your Internet provider (Comcast, AT&T etc.).
- Your cell phone provider.
- Websites you visit.
- Your email provider (Google, Yahoo, Microsoft, and Apple) can read your emails. Yes, all of them reserve the right to do so.
- Your employer tracks what you do on their systems, or any systems that have been authorized to log in to their network.
- Public places such as schools and libraries usually have tracking software (for safety, adult content, etc.).
- Any of your neighbors if you don't have a password on your WiFi network.
- Social networks (Facebook, etc.).
- Many apps, especially those that have online features.
- I assume the government probably tracks everything.
- As an old X-Files fan I can assure you the aliens are also tracking.

So let's cover the more mundane, how to clear your search and browsing history.

Delete Search History

How to delete Google search history, note Google will keep storing it unless you turn it off (very easy to do). Most people choose to delete all but you can just delete recent items or sort though it. Easy wins, just delete it all. This works across all your devices, you don't have to do it on each one (assuming your Google sync is working).

Delete Google history **(Chrome IE Win\Mac\Android\iPhone):**
1. https://history.google.com/history/.
2. Settings gear (at top right).
3. Choose **Settings**.
4. Go to the **Account History** tab.
5. Sometimes you have to click Account History twice to see everything. If you only see Search you're not seeing everything.
6. There are several areas you can check with **Manage History.**
7. Most areas including **Things you search for** let you select all and then delete.
8. For **Places you've been** (Google maps etc.) the delete is on the left side.

Turn off Search History

To turn off Google history **(Chrome IE Win\MAC\Android\iPhone):**
1. At the Account History tab from above.
2. Click it again to make sure all items show up.
3. There is a **Pause** button in each area.
4. Click on it and then click on **Pause History** to confirm.

Google tips on turning off or deleting search history:
- https://support.google.com/websearch/answer/465?hl=en

Delete Browser History

Clearing your browser history in Chrome is supposed to clear it on all your devices you are logged into. However, I have found that this does not always work. So I would recommend you do this on each device to be sure.

To delete browsing history **(Chrome for Win\Mac):**
1. Chrome menu (three bars top right), also called hotdog.
2. **History**.
3. If you log in to more than one device (phone\tablet etc.) you

should also see the history on those devices as well.
4. Click on the **Clear Browsing Data** button.
5. Choose **from the beginning of time** on the pull-down menu.
6. Generally you want the following checked.
7. **Browsing History, Download History, Cookies, Cached images.**
8. Checking Cookies will impact two-step verification if you are using it. You will just have to check remember this device again, the next time you login.
9. Click on the **Clear Browsing** button at the bottom.

Additional information:
- It may take two or three minutes to clear the history.
- You might notice that Chrome runs faster (this is a happy thing).

Google tips on privacy settings **(Chrome)**:
https://support.google.com/chrome/answer/114836?hl=en

To delete browsing history **(IE for Windows)**:
1. Assuming you have the menu visible (always a good idea).
2. **Tools**.
3. **Delete Browser History**.
4. Generally you should have the following checked.
5. **Preserve Favorites, Temporary Internet files, Cookies, History, Download History**.
6. **Delete** (the defaults that are checked should be fine).

Microsoft gets an A for how easy this is.

Microsoft tips on Browser History **(IE)**:
- http://windows.microsoft.com/en-us/internet-explorer/manage-delete-browsing-history-internet-explorer#ie=ie-11

To delete browsing history **(Chrome for Android Phone)**:
1. **Menu** button.
2. **Settings**.
3. **Privacy**.

4. **Clear Browsing data** (at the bottom).
5. Generally you should have the following items checked.
6. **Clear browsing history, Clear the cache, Clear Cookies**
7. Click **Clear** to confirm.
8. Press the Back key twice to return to web.

To delete browsing history **(Chrome for iPhone)**:
1. Menu three bars (also called Hot Dog).
2. History.
3. Clear Browsing History.
4. Click **Clear Browsing Data** (at the bottom).
5. **Clear Browsing History**
6. **Clear Browsing History** (with the trashcan to confirm)

Turn Off Browser History

To turn off browser history **(Chrome for Windows <u>not easy</u>)**:
1. Add a new tab in Incognito mode. You have to do this every time, it's not automatic.
2. Chrome menu (three bars top right), also called hotdog.
3. **New Incognito window**.
Or the complicated way, and if you make a mistake Chrome may not work.
1. First copy the item or shortcut you use to launch Chrome and paste a second version (in case you make a mistake).
2. Edit the properties on the application file or shortcut by adding –incognito at the end (somewhat complicated, steps below).
3. Right-click the properties of the application icon for Chrome.
4. Under Target, go to the very end and add a space and then – incognito and save.
5. It should look something like this.
6. "C:\Program Files (x86)\Google\Chrome\Application\chrome.exe" – incognito
7. Every time you start chrome from this icon it will be in incognito mode (the man with the hat always shows up).

To turn off browser history **(IE for Windows most versions)**:

1. Assuming you have the menu visible (always a good idea), **Tools.**
2. **Internet Options.**
3. **General** tab.
4. Under **Browsers History.**
5. Click **Settings.**
6. **History** tab.
7. **Days to keep pages in History** set to 0.
8. OK.
9. OK.

Microsoft gets another A for how easy this is.

Turn off browser history **(Chrome for Mac):**
- There is no easy way to do this on a Mac. If anyone knows a good (must be simple) way to do this, let me know.
- Locking the History file under Library/Application Support/Google/Chrome/Default may not be a good idea. It may cause issues with updates and or break Chrome in some unexpected way.

Turn off browser history **(Chrome for Android and Chrome for iPhone):**
- The only easy way to do this is use Incognito mode.
- If anyone has an easy way (no hacks) to do this let me know.

Tip #44
Take a look at museums maps.

Google has mapped a number of museums and it's like a remote field trip. If you're doing any research on museums, it's worth taking it for a spin.

Speaking of field tips, there's a great Google app with the same name, the next time you're on the road check it out. They have added non historical landmarks and references in recent years, however, it's still a great educational app.

Museums maps:
https://www.google.com/maps/views/streetview/art-project?gl=us

Tip #45
Use maps and Google Earth.

If you're searching for a place, there is no better choice than to pull it up within Google Maps. It gives you a great feel for the location and environment. Many times a search might be better done in maps. Sometimes a search will open to maps because it thinks (and is often correct) that a map search would be best.

If you are looking for a restaurant, typing the word restaurant in maps will highlight everything near you, the same for shoe stores etc. Maps itself could cover a whole separate set of tips, but here are a few of my favorites. Except for the last 2 tips for sending location, they should work the same across all devices.

Google Map Search Tips:
- Zooming in will always give local details such as shops and businesses.
- Typing in what you're looking for generically such as restaurant will show you all of them. Typing in Starbucks will show you all the nearby locations.
- If you click on a venue such as a concert theater, it often gives upcoming events at the bottom of the pop-up. Click on it and it should give you even more events.
- You can search for public transportation schedules which comes in very handy. Click on Transit (looks like a bus) and enter your destination and it will give you the schedules.
- If you want to share an address or location (Only works on phones and tablets at this time), just press on the location until a pin shows up. The address will show below the map, scroll down a bit and you can share the location. A good example is pick me up here. If you send it as a text message, the person who gets it, clicks on it and it should open Maps with directions on how to get there.
- Although I love the send location feature on Google maps

my son still prefers Android GPS Share by Ken Kinder

Map tips from Googles (note mobile tips are at the bottom):
https://support.google.com/maps/?hl=en#topic=3092425

Tip #46
When <u>not</u> to use Maps and Google Earth.

For all its great and cool features you should not try to use your phones mapping program when you are camping or outdoors. It works differently than a standalone GPS. It needs to connect to your phone carrier to work. Although you can download some part of Google maps or a specific GPS app, it's not something that you can count on.

So, if you are going hiking and want the added security of a GPS, purchase a stand-alone GPS device. Preferably one that takes standard batteries so you can carry spares.

Tip #47
Search for Images.

Sometimes you just want to find a picture or image. It could be a famous work of art or an image. Google offers a few different methods to do this. One uses an extension for Chrome and I'm not a fan of extensions and browser add-ons. I know there are many great extensions out there and at one time I reviewed over 400 Firefox extensions. The trend is away from extensions and I am trying to keep it as simple as possible for these examples.

Google does a great job of reviewing the methods to search for an image; however I generally copy the image URL. Of course if you're using Chrome all you have to do is right-click on an image and select Search Google for this image.

To use Chrome for an image search:

1. Right-click the image.
2. Choose **Search Google for this image**.

To use Chrome's image search copy URL method:
1. Right-click the image.
2. **Copy Image URL**.
3. Go to the website
4. http://images.google.com/.
5. Paste into the search box.
6. For better matches click **Search by Image** (top left).

Image Search tips from Google:
http://www.google.com/insidesearch/features/images/searchbyimage.html

Image Search alternative (TinEye):
https://www.tineye.com/

Tip #48
Search with your camera.

I did say that search is changing. Yes, if you have a Smartphone it has a number of options to search by taking a picture. There is even a Real Estate app that will give you the house price by just taking a picture. There are too many apps to even list that scan or search or even translate with your camera, so check out the app store.

Initially, some of the more popular search apps were barcode scanners. You could just go online or to a store and scan the bar code and it would give you detailed information including prices. You can still do this, but many companies use their own bar codes or have special codes just for their store. This diminished the usability of the apps, but it's free and it only takes a minute to try.

If you are using the Google Now (more tips coming next), it has an option to search by camera. Also, Google Goggles (Android).

To use Google Now's Search by Camera:
1. Camera menu.

2. **Settings**.
3. Touch **Search from Camera**.
4. Check the **Search from Camera** box.

Google Search by Camera option information:
https://support.google.com/websearch/answer/186334?hl=en

Tip #49
Find some good phone apps (Google can't be great at everything).

Searching is good, almost magical these days. However, it sometimes can't compete with a great app dedicated to providing you with specific information. Hey I live in California and love Earthquake Alert! by Josh Clemm (Android only), I haven't found anything else that comes close. If you're searching for medical information WebMD is a great app that can quickly give you lots of great info.

I have an Android Galaxy and iPhone and have installed more apps then I care to admit (mostly on the Galaxy). I try to keep it under 500 on the Galaxy but I did cross the 1,200 barrier before I started to pair it down.

So checking out the app stores from time to time may help you discover a great app that puts Google to shame in a specific area. No search provider can be the best at everything.

Here's a quick list of some of the best apps, some are only on Android, and I am leaving off the obvious such as Facebook etc. Sorry a few are geeky. This is just a quick list, otherwise I'd spend 2 weeks trying to organize it and delay these search tips. My advice if you are short on time (we all are), find a good inspirational app to make your day go better. I have listed two in the beginning, when you have more time, explore the rest.

Another note on Safety. The Apple store is safe and the applications have been carefully screened, the same is true for the Google Play store. However, there are other places you can get Android apps, I would not recommend getting Android apps from anywhere else than Google Play, the Amazon app store or Samsung app store if you have a Samsung phone.

50 cool & interesting Android apps (many are also for iPhone):
Inspirational Quotes Free (by Vankiros), Motivational Quote for Success (by Piapps), Twilight (the app not the movie, to get rid of that blue light and sleep better), TED, Fireworks, Talking Tom, Magic Fluids, KidsDoodle (good to have some fun kids apps, they can save the day), Google Sky Maps, Moon 3D, 3D UFO (let's all be paranoid), Google Field Trip, GPS Share, Spotify, projectM (cool screen effects based on the music playing), IMDb, Netflix, Share Apps (by Squid Tooth) Pandora, Fandango, iFunny (be careful it's a time waster), Digg, Meetup, Kindle Reader, Zing (See who's on your network and more), Earth Quake Alert (by Josh), Red Cross First Aid (there are many great Red Cross apps), WebMD, Google Hangouts, Hangouts Dialer, Speed Test (by OOKLA), Quick Pic, Remote Desktop, Google Keep (Great for notes and to-do lists), Zillow, Paper Camera, Gas Buddy, Mint, Google Drive, Disk Usage (by Ivan Volosyuk, great way to see the space on your Android phone), ES File Explorer, List my apps, AIO Toolbox, Antutu, Google Photos, Network Signal Info, Barcode Scanner (by ZXing Team), BART Usher (for the SF bay area), Google Device Manager, Torque (also need $15-$40 Bluetooth adapter to read auto codes).

Tip #50
Google Now commands (also called Google Search App – yes, it's confusing).

As I mentioned in the beginning, the search bar is also becoming the command bar. So it might get a little confusing and you should start to know some of the Google Now commands for voice input. All search commands start with "Search for" however it is a Google Now command and should help Google understand what you want to search for.

These commands are starting to integrate with apps making them even more powerful, but also potentially confusing. There can be minor differences on how these work in Android, iPhones, Chrome OS, and Chrome Browser on Windows or Mac computers.

Google Now Command examples
- **Search for** (Tells Google that you want so search).
- **Remind me to** (Set a reminder such as buy milk).
- **Wake me up** (Sets the alarm).
- **Note to self** (Posts to Keep, Evernote and other apps).
- **Call** (Places call).
- **Navigate to** (Uses map to get directions).
- **Browse to** (Opens a web page).
- **What's this song** (Works the same as Shazam).

Google Now main support page:
https://support.google.com/websearch/topic/4409793?rd=1

Google Now brief overview:
https://support.google.com/websearch/answer/2819496?hl=en&ref_topic=6032673

Extra Tip
An extra tip, just for fun, (in case you're really good at search and get asked for help).

We started with a little fun and we can end this way. Sometimes you might get asked a very simple question, one that can easily be looked up in Google. There's a website just for that; **Let Me Google That For You** with a simple web address, LMGTFY.COM.

If you get asked a question, you can type it into the website and it will provide a link. You can send someone the link which Googles the question and provides the answers. Check it out; it will help prove that you really know how to search, even with a fancy trick. Note this website is not part of Google.

Tell me what you think.

Hopefully you learned a few new tips. Please let me know your favorite tips and any I may have missed. I hope to update these tips by late 2015 and will include as much feedback as possible.

Thanks
Tom

Feeback50Searchtips@gmail.com

50 Tips para una Búsqueda Simple y Segura

Enero 2015

De la Serie *Tech Simple and Easy*

Thomas Lahey

DEDICATORIA

A todos y cada uno de quienes tratan de hacer la vida un poco mas fácil
para el resto de nosotros.

CONTENIDO

INTRODUCTION

Para simplificar me enfocaré en el proveedor de Búsquedas más popular, Google, por supuesto. También me enfocaré en los browsers Chrome e Internet Explorer (IE). Aunque creo que hay buenas razones para usar sólo Chrome o IE, lo mismo no es verdad para la búsqueda Google. Si prefieres Bing o Yahoo para las búsquedas, está bien. Muchos de los tips se aplican aún cuando usas estos proveedores.

Páginas de soporte para Microsoft Bing;
- http://onlinehelp.microsoft.com/en-us/bing
- http://onlinehelp.microsoft.com/en-us/bing/ff808438.aspx

Páginas de soporte para Yahoo Search;
- https://help.yahoo.com/kb/search

He usado Google por varios años y concnozco mi parte de trucos y tips. De cualquier modo, es difícil mantenerse actualizado. Esto también hace difícil encontrar documentacion actualizada a la fecha. El sueño son aplicaciones que necesiten documentación minima, y que podamos utilizar intuitiva y naturalmente. Quizás llegue el día cuando tips, trucos y hojas de trampa sean cosas del pasado. Sólo nos queda esperar.

Aquí presento mis tips para la Búsqueda en Google para Enero 2015, después de revisar mi tips algo obsoletos. Lo triste es que hace unos años había muchas más y mejores referencias al respecto. Había posters de Google para las clases. Tal vez ahora se asume que todos sabemos realizar búsquedas y es tan intuitivo que no hay necesidad de materiales de referencia. La Búsqueda en sí misma está evolucionando y algunos elementos están cambiando y se están transfiriendo a apps (ver la seccion Qué hay de Nuevo en 2015). De cualquier modo, aún hay tips muy buenos que no todos conocen y espero que usted encontre vaios aquí.
Como las cosas cambian a menudo, estoy seguro que en pocos meses por lo menos un set de pasos se volverán obsoletos. Espero que el cambio sea mínimo y sea fácil para usted encontrar los nuevos pasos.

El ritmo de cambios especialmente en los Browsers está comenzando a crecer. Contar con actualizaciones automáticas es muy seguro. Sin embargo, usted puede notar que algunos de los menús o settings serán diferentes a los que recuerda. Usted no está perdiendo la razón, son los constantes canbios del mundo tecnológico.

Tuve que añadir algunos tips para asegurar que su experiencia de Búsquedas la esperada. Los primeros tips aseguran que Chrome e IE trabajen apropiadamente y no estén utilizando una malvada barra de herramientas añadida (sé que no todas las barras de herramientas son malvadas). Tampoco se puede pensar en Búsquedas sin pensar en protección, por eso tambien incluyo tips para eso.

NUEVO PARA 2015

Un gran cambio está llegando para las Búsquedas y usted puede no saber que ya está en el horizonte. Hace años íbamos a Google.com para hacer las Búsquedas. Ahora la mayoría sabe que puede realizar búsquedas tan sólo tipeando en la barra de URL en la parte superior del Browser. Esto facilita las cosas. Aún puede ir a Google.com y realizar búsquedas, y usar opciones avanzadas (cubierto más adelante).

Lo que es nuevo, son los asistentes de voz, Siri, Google Now, y Cortana. En un comienzo se utilizaron prinicpalmente para Búsqueda por voz. Sin embargo, hoy permiten comandos tales como despiértame (wake-me-up) para ordenar al teléfono que programe una alarma. Estos comandos tienen su propia sintaxis (formatos y palabras clave), pero se ingresan en la barra de Búsquedas o utilizando el micrófono opcional.

Veo donde algunos pueden confundirse. Si usted tipea o dice "despiértame" buscando canciones de Evanescence, no se sorprenda si en lugar de ello, su teléfono responde queriendo programar una alarma.

Si todos los comandos comenzaran con la palabra "Buscar" sería muy claro, pero no es el caso. En el futuro cercano usted debe conocer estos comandos para evitar confusiones. Hay algunos tips y links para Google Now al final del libro.

Esto recae en "Tengo que mantenerme al día con la tecnología o ya no voy a entender como usarrlo". Esperemos que todo lo nuevo que logramos hacer con la tecnología ayude a aliviar la molestia constante de mantenernos actualizados con su uso.

Comencemos con algunos puntos clave y un compendio de los mejores tips.

Algunos puntos clave;
- Los tips relacionados con la seguridad y protección cambiarán con el tiempo pero no se vuelven menos importantes.
- Al mejorar el Buscador, algunos de estos tips pierden utilidad (Quotes, Exclude, Wildcards), pero ésto es bueno al final.
- El Buscador y Asistentes de Voz como Siri y Google Now se están combinando, esto impacta la manera en que usted usa el Buscador y sus dispositivos.
- Chrome es el único Browser que se encuentra en todas las mayores plataformas (Win, Mac, Android, iPhone), y es muy bueno. Por lo tanto es lo que usted debería usar. Internet Explorer (IE) gana en seguridad para niños, pero requiere entender y manejar cuentas de Window.
- Si usted no ha escuchado acerca de la verificación de dos pasos, revísela.
- Si usted es un estudiante o no ha usado Google Académico, pruébelo, especialmente el link de citas debajo de cada resultado.
- Considere comprar un Chromebook, es lo que la mayoría necesita, y hace la vida **mucho más fácil.** Tienen unas pocas limitaciones pero su precio es razonable. Algunas personas me dicen que no la adquieren porque no tiene Skype, sin embargo Google Hangouts es una gran alternativa para Skype.

Para ustedes, los que quieren ir directamente al punto (hey, todos somos impacientes) estos son los 10 tips más estupendos. Déjenme saber si estan de acuerdo.

Los Mejores Tips

- # 1 Comience con tips y juegos divertidos
- # 2 Manténgase Seguro, usa la versión vigente del Browser y anti-virus.
- # 7 Use el browser Chrome.
- # 9 Use la verificación de dos pasos.
- #23 Use opciones avanzadas de Búsqueda en Google.
- #31 Busque el horario de la cartelera en Google, clean no movie adds.
- #36 Use Google Académico para investigar y facilitar citaciones.
- #40 Customice Google search, cree su propia búsqueda.
- #43 Busque y navegue en la red de manera anónima.
- #50 Comandos de Google Now y Búsqueda por voz.

Para todos los demas, e incluso para los lectores impacientes, estos son todos los tips.

Tip #1
Un poco de diversión para comenzar.

Hoy en día hay un poco más de diversion en la tecnología, quizás con la intención de opacar las cosas que nos sacan de quicio. Estos son tips y trucos divertidos para la Búsqueda de Google. Algunos tips como estos se volvieron obsoletos porque Google cambia el uso de resultados automáticos. Es difícil mantenerse actualizado.

- En Google busque **tilt**.
- En Google busque **do a barrel roll**.
- En Google busque (sqrt(cos(x))*cos(400*x)+sqrt (abs(x))-0.4)*(4-x*x)^0.1 (quién dice que los matemáticos no tienen sentimientos).
- Busque **fun google tips**.
- Vaya a Google Doodles (www.google.com/doodles).

Tip #2
Manténgase seguro y actualizado.

Desearía que todo lo referente a seguridad y protección en línea fuera más simple, lo bueno es que los esfuerzos para mejorar la seguridad son continuos. Este es un resumen de los puntos que cubro y algunos links clave;

Acceso en linea para niños (tips específicos a seguir);
- Nunca permita a niños el acceso a la Internet sin supervisión.
- IE (10 ó mayor es lo mejor) con el filtro familiar activado.
- Use Google como su proveedor de búsquedas.
- Habilite Google Safe Search.
- Asegúrese de que su computadora esté actualizada.
- Asegúrese de que su browser sea moderno.
- Instale un prograna antivirus actualizado.
- No asuma que los sitios públicos, como las bibliotecas, son 100% seguras.

Algunos links:
- https://kids.usa.gov/online-safety/index.shtml
- https://www.onguardonline.gov/articles/0006-talk-your-kids
- http://www.nationalcac.org/prevention/internet-safety-kids.html

Algunos de los tips que siguen, cubren varios de los ítems anteriores. Para manteerse al día, anote los links (bookmark) y consúltelos regularmente para estar informado de las novedades.

Tip #3
Para niños pequeños, sólo use el Buscador Google.

Estos son algunos lugares donde se utilizan filtros de información:
- A nivel de Redes, para escuelas, bibliotecas, compañías.
- A nivel se Sistema Operativo (OS) de computadoras o tabletas.
- Software filtros antivirus, etc.

- Browsers (IE, Chrome, Firefox, etc.) dependiendo de los settings.
- El proveedor del Buscador que se use, Google, Bing, Yahoo.

Google, Bing, y Yahoo tienen diferentes modos de búsqueda. La diferencia principal es que Google generalmente filtra un gran contenido adulto de manera automática. De todos los poderes que tiene su Buscador, Goggle ha decidido que el contenido adulto no va a ser uno de ellos.

No asuma que no puede encontrar contenido adulto usando Google search, pero la probabilidad de que éste accidentalmente se muestre, especialmente fotos, es mucho menor. Todos cometemos errores de tipeo y no queremos sorpresas desagradables.

Para setear Google como su proveedor para Chrome:
1. Seleccione **Menu > Settings > Search**.
2. Escoja **Google** del menú.

Para setear Google como su proveedor en la mayoría de las versiones de Intenet Explorer:
1. Seleccione **Tools > Manager Add-ons >Search Providers**.
2. Resalte **Google**.
3. Seleccione **Set as Default** (derecho, abajo).
4. Seleccione **Close**.

Asegurarse que esté realmente utilizando Google Search es más laborioso de lo que usted piensa. Es muy común que los hackers intercepten Browsers y la gente a menudo realiza búsquedas en la barra URL sin visitar Google.com. Por favor lea el tip para resetear su navegador.

Tip #4
Use Google Safe Search.

Google tiene sus propios settings para búsquedas que se usan sin importar cuál sea su navegador. Usted debería usarlo en adición a otros programas de seguridad.

Es fácil setearlo y le permite enlazarlo a su cuenta.

Para activar Google Safe Search en su navegador:
1. Vaya a http://www.google.com/preferences.
2. Chequee la caja **Filter explicit results**.
3. Usted puede fijar SafeSearch, pero esto requiere accesar a una cuenta de Google para que funcione.

Información sobre SafeSearch:
https://support.google.com/websearch/answer/510?hl=en

Tip #5
Para niños pequeños, considere usar Internet Explorer.

Me agrada mucho Chrome, pero a pesar de sus ventajas, carece de filtros de seguridad básicos. Estoy seguro que Chrome tendrá filtros mejorados pronto pero actualmente Internet Explorer (IE) le lleva ventaja. Si un niño pequeño está usando el buscador Google o simplemente está en línea, considere usar IE versión 10 o mayor. Por supuesto los niños menores no deben accesar a Internet sin supervisión. Las escuelas y las bibliotecas generalmente tienen filtros, pero nada es 100% seguro.

Las versiones de IE se complican y en algunos casos usted no puede actualizarlo a IE 10 u 11, pero varias versiones iniciales soportan las aplicaciones de seguridad familiar (Family Safety feature).

Para setear la seguridad de IE en la mayoría de versiones:
1. **Tools**.
2. **Internet Options**.
3. **Content**.
4. **Family Safety**.

Usted podría encontrarse con una solicitud de cuenta de nuevo usuario, o ser informado de que su cuenta es la del Administrador cuando accede a Seguridad Familiar (Family Safety). Si éste es el caso y usted no entiende completamente cómo setear una cuenta y los permisos de Windows, encuentre a alguien que lo asista o saltee este paso. No quisiera que usted fuera sacado de Windows.

Información de Microsoft sobre seguridad en línea:
- http://windows.microsoft.com/en-US/windows-8/family-safety
- http://www.microsoft.com/security/family-safety/childsafety-age.aspx

Tip #6
Seteo apropiado para computadoras compartidas con niños.

Muchas computadoras se comparten entre varias personas. Un tip simple es que los niños usen IE con las opciones de Seguridad Familiar (Family Safety Feature). Todos pueden usar Chrome u otro navegador que no está en el Menú principal, o en las pestañas, etc.

- Una computadora usada por niños debe tener todas las aplicaciones de Seguridad activadas.
- Otro método es "no" proveer la clave de la computadora a los niños. Esto garantiza saber cuándo ellos entran a la Internet.

Tip #7
Use el navegador Chrome (mayormente).

Sí, esto viene después del tip que recomienda usar IE para niños pequeños. Como muchas cosas en la vida, la misma solución no funciona para todo. En general, Chrome es el mejor navegador y lo recomiendo grandemente con excepción para niños pequeños. Asumo que a los jóvenes se les hace muy fácil encontrar la manera de evadir filtros y límites. Sí, es un mundo agresivo, y los desafíos son más grandes que nunca.

Para simplificar, use Chrome.

Desde que Apple dejó los navegadores Window, no ha habido competencia. Sólo hay un jugador que tiene un navegador en todas las plataformas, Google Chrome. Probablemente Microsoft nunca tendrá una versión completa de IE para iPhone o IE para Androides. El IE Remoto es una solución pobre.

Chrome debe trabajar en el 99% de páginas web sin importar en qué dispositivo (teléfono, tableta, o computadora). Chrome también tiene grandes aplicaciones que funcionan con la búsqueda de Google y con apps Google. Aún hay diferencias menores entre Chrome en sus diferentes plataformas (Windows, Mac, y Androide).

Tip #8
Regístrese en Google para usar Chrome.

Si su computadora, teléfono y tableta son usados sólo por usted, es muy fácil, sólo acceda a su cuenta Google:

Para acceder a Google:
1. **Menu**.
2. **Settings**
3. **Sign in**
4. Ingrese su cuenta

Acceder a Google le brinda beneficios tales como la sincronización de Chrome en todos sus dispositivos. Los ítems, tales como bookmarks, funcionan en todos sus dispositivos. Recuerde que Chrome soporta usuarios multiples, lo cual se vuelve un poco confuso. Cuando usted accede a Google, éste recuerda sus búsquedas y eso ayuda en sus búsquedas futuras. A algunas personas les gusta esto, a otras no. Si usted no quiere ser reconocido en sus búsquedas, hay un tip más adelante para hacer búsquedas de manera anónima.

Si varias personas usan una computadora, cada una de ellas puede acceder a Google usando su propia cuenta. La confusión se genera cuando una persona olvida esto y usa la computadora accediendo a la cuenta de otra persona. Por precaución es mejor no ingresar con Chrome a una computadora compartida.

Tip #9
Use la verificación de dos pasos para ingresar.

Esta verificación no está relacionada directamente con las búsquedas, pero si está usted trabajando en una cuenta Google o Apple, debería usarla. Lo que esto significa es que usted necesita más de una clave para entrar a su cuenta. Usted necesita un código de uno de sus otros dispositivios, teléfono, tableta, etc. El código cambia todo el tiempo, haciendo casi imposible que un hacker acceda a su cuenta.

Hay algunas diferencias clave en la manera en que esta doble verificación funciona en Apple y Google, y el proceso puede ser un poco confuso. No cubro todos los pasos aquí pero proveo unos enlaces que pueden ayudar.

- Para Apple, su teléfono obtiene un codigo de confirmación cucando usted trata de ingresar a su cuenta. Usted necesita ese código para ingresar. Usted puede ajustar los settings para que su dispositivo sea reconocido.
- Para Google, después de la primera vez que usted ingresa un código, usted puede indicar a Google que recuerde su teléfono, o su tableta, y no necesitará un código nuevo otra vez. Cada vez que un dispositivo nuevo intenta acceder a su cuenta, Google requeriá el código por lo menos la primera vez.
- En Google, la doble verificación usa cookies para recordar si usted no desea que se requerira un código nuevamente en ese dispositivo. Si usted aclara sus cookies, usted requerirá un código otra vez para ingresar.
- Además, si usted usa esta verificación de dos pasos, y tiene Google Hangouts como su app de mensajes default, esto es un problema. Su cuenta de Hangouts podría bloquearse a la espera de un password, pero usted sólo lo puede obtener de

Hangouts. Tuve un episodio divertido con esto una vez.
- Google está avanzando más allá de esta verificación hacia un Sistema integrado entre todos sus dispositivos, siempre seguro pero sin requerir siempre un código de dos pasos.
- Google también tiene códigos backup para esta verificación de dos pasos.

Algunos links sobre verificación de Dos Pasos (Two-Step):
- http://www.google.com/landing/2step/
- http://support.apple.com/kb/ht5570

Con los recientes hacks a las cuentas de actrices famosas Apple está tratando de hacer algunas actualizaciones necesarias a su seguridad, esperemos que eso continúe.

Tip #10
Asegúrese de que Chrome e Internet Explorer estén actualizados.

Para versiones recientes de Chrome esto no es un problema porque en ellas la actualización es automática. Si por alguna razón usted tiene una versión antigua, es fácil arreglarlo. Primero, si usted ve el menú de tres barars arriba a la derecha, de color verde, anaranjado o rojo, esto significa que Chrome está desactualizado. Si usted ve una herramienta, una llave inglesa, en la esquina superior derecha, usted está usando una versión antigua (la llave inglesa se cambió por las tres barras en el 2012). Cuando el menú esta resaltado en color, entonces **Update Google Chrome** debe mostrarse bajo el menú. Usted tal vez tenga que reinicializar Chrome después de esta actualización.

Actualización de Chrome:
1. Menú (tres barras a la derecha superior), llamado también hotdog.
2. **About Google Chrome**.
3. **Google Chrome is up to date** debe estar marcado como chequeado, si no, seleccione **Update Google Chrome**. En la mayoría de los casos no es necesario reiniciar Chrome.

Para versiones actuales de Internet Explorer (IE) tampoco es un problema. IE se <u>actualiza automáticamente.</u> Usted debe tener la actualzación de Windows seteada como automática de manera que todas las actualizaciones y aplicaciones de seguidad sean automáticamente instaladas.

Para instalar las actualizaciones para la mayoría de versiones IE:
1. **Help**.
2. **About Internet Explorer**.
3. **Install new versions automatically** (debe estar marcado como chequeado).

Tip #11
Resetee Chrome o IE a su seteo default.

Sí, aun Chrome no está a salvo de hacks de navegadores. Le tomó a Google "demasiado tiempo" pero Chrome ahora tiene la capacidad de resetearse. Esto no es una opción para Chrome en teléfonos, y actualmente no hay muchas aplicaciones para teléfonos, de manera que usted está relativamente protegido por ahora. Si el navegador de su computadora ha sido ya hackeado, a menudo es el área de búsquedas la que ha sido afectada, y usted necesita resetear.

En cualquier caso, resetear Chrome es una buena idea.

El reseteo limpia todo excepto las claves archivadas, bookmarks y el motor de las busquedas personalizadas (tips sobre esto más adelante). Si usted usa cualquier extensión, el reseteo sólo las apagará, y usted podrá encenderlas nuevamente.

Para resetear Chrome (Windows, Mac):
1. Manú Chrome (tres barras arriba derecha), llamado también hotdog.
2. **Settings** (ir al pie).
3. **Show Advanced Settings** (otra vez al pie).
4. **Reset Settings**.

Usted puede notar que Chrome es más rápido (esto es algo bueno).

Información sobre reseteo de Chrome:
https://support.google.com/chrome/answer/3296214?p=ui_reset_settings&rd=1

Resetear IE es un poco más complicado ya que éste **resetea los setting de seguridad y protección**, de manera que usten tiene que reconfigurarlos nuevamente. **Si usted ya tiene la aplicación de Seguridad Familiar activada, no le recomiendo resetear IE**. Si todo esto es nuevo para usted, entonces sí resetee IE, y luego añada la aplicaciones de seguridad familiar.

Para resetear IE (la mayoría de versiones)
1. **Tools**.
2. **Internet Options**.
3. **Advanced** tab.
4. **Reset**.
5. **Tools**.
6. **Internet**.
7. **Options**.
8. **Content**.
9. **Family Safety**.

Otra vez, a usted se le podría requerir setear una nueva cuenta de usuario, o ser informado de que su cuenta es la cuenta del Administrador cuando accesa a Seguridad Familiar (Family Safety). Si éste es el caso, y usted no entiende completamente como instalar cuentas y permisos en Windows, busque ayuda o saltee este paso. Es una aplicación, pero no quisiera que usted fuera retirado del ambiente Windows. Me encantaría que Microsoft tuviera la opción de tan sólo usar una clave para accesar a la aplicación de Seguirdad Familiar.

Información de reseteo para Microsoft IE:
support.microsoft.com/kb/923737

Tip #12
Haga Google su motor de Búsqueda default.

Para Chrome en computadoras Windows o Macs si usted siguió el tip anterior, todo esta bien. Si por alguna razón usted no reseteó Chrome o desea asegurarse de que esté correcto en su teléfono o tableta, aquí están los pasos.

Para setear Google como herramienta de Búsqueda default en Chrome o Windows:
1. Menú – tres barras arriba, derecha (conocido como hot dog).
2. **Settings**.
3. **Search**.
4. **Manage Search Engines**.
5. Elija Google como Default.
6. **Done**.

Para setear Google como herramienta de Búsqueda default en Chrome en una Mac:
1. Menú – tres barras arriba, derecha (hot dog).
2. **Settings**.
3. **Search**.
4. **Manage Search Engines**.
5. Elija Google como Default.
6. **Done**.

Para setear Google como herramienta de Búsquedas default en un iPhone:
1. Menú – tres barras arriba, derecha (hot dog).
2. **Settings**.
3. **Search Engine**.
4. **Google**.
5. **Done**.

Para setear Google como herramienta de Búsquedas default en un teléfono Androide:
1. Use el botón de menú al pie.
2. **Settings**.
3. **Search engine**
4. Seleccione Google.

Para setear Google como herramienta de Búsquedas default en la mayoría de versiones IE:

1. **Tools**.
2. **Manage Add-ons**.
3. **Search Providers**.
4. Resalte Google.
5. **Set as Default** si todavía no está (derecha, abajo).
6. **Close**.

Tip #13
Use un programa antivirus.

Lamentable esto es confuso para Windows, porque cuando usted compra una computadora, ésta ya tiene un produco antivirus instalado con una fecha de expiración cercana (a veces de 60 a 90 días). Usted debe tener un solo producto antivirus trabajando en su computadora, por eso el programa propio de Microsoft ha sido apagado. La compañía del programa antivirus pagó para que hicieran eso, y no es una buena situación.

Las computadoras Apple traen un softwate antivirus instalado que funciona por default y es gratis y muy bueno. Si usted quiere comprar algo más, hay varias opciones. Los Chromebooks no necesitan software antivirus, una de las muchas razones para comprar uno; esperemos que eso no cambie.

La mayoría de programas antivirus para Windows requieren una subscripción y pagos anuales para continuar funcionando, lo cual no es muy bueno.

La otra opción es determinar cómo retirar el programa que vino con su computadora Windows e instalar algo diferente con opciones gratis que incluyan el programa antivirus de Microsoft (Security Essentials para Windows 7 y Windows Defender para Windows 8). **Si usted conoce a alguien que lo ayude, está con suerte.**

Para Windows 8 (y Windows 10 que ya llega), la buena noticia es que usted no tiene que instalar Windows defender. Está colococado automáticamente y **no puede ser retirado**. Puede ser deshabilitado, y esto ocurre cuando otro programa antivirus es instalado. De nuevo, usted no puede tener más de un programa antivirus operando al mismo tiempo.

Tengo sentimientos mezclados ante qué recomendar para Windows debido a esto. El software antivirus gratis de Microsoft no es el primero en el ranking de protección, pero se actualiza automáticamente y es gratis.

Mi sugerencia es que si usted no es muy bueno con las computadoras y no conoce a alguien que pueda ayudarlo, compre **cuidadosamente** la licencia para usar el antivirus que vino con la computadora.

Si usted invierte $1,400 en un sistema y el dinero no es un problema para usted, compre el paquete antivirus de lujo. Si usted compra una conputadora por $300 y $200 extra es más de lo que puede afrontar, sólo compre el antivirus básico ($20-$40). Otra opción es comprar un Chromebook, que hace lo que la mayoría de la gente necesita por un precio fantástico y no necesita un programa antivirus. No quiero sugerir la "Mejor" tienda, pero hay una que lo es, donde generalmente usted puede realizar la mejor compra luego de recibir buenos consejos cuando va a adquirir una computadora. Ellos por supuesto, van a querer vender el programa antivirus más costoso.

Información de Chromebook:
http://www.google.com/intl/en/chrome/devices/features/

Tip #14
Use las páginas de soporte deGoogle.

Google tiene sus propias páginas de búsqueda que contienen grandes tips. Sólo sepa que Google como otros, tiene mucho material de referencia, que cambia a menudo. Ocasionalmente algunos tips están un poco obsoletos. De manera que debería ser ell 99%.

Dedique unos minutos a estas páginas y estará listo para dominar Search. Debido a que son Búsquedas de Google, Patent Search, Scholar, Google Now, y más, no todo se encuentra en los links a continuación. Cubro estas búsquedas especializadas en mis tips e incluyo links en cada tip, entonces por favor continue leyendo.

Soporte de Google search:
- http://www.google.com/insidesearch/
- http://www.google.com/insidesearch/tipstricks/
- http://www.google.com/insidesearch/tipstricks/all.html
- http://www.google.com/insidesearch/searcheducation/index.html

Tip #15
Busque directamente en la barra URL de su browser.

En caso de que usted no lo sepa, la manera más fácil de hacer búsquedas es tipear directamente en la barra URL de su navegador. Esto funciona con todos los navegadores. Si con sus resultados usted recibe mucha propaganda o alguna otra cosa que no le sirva vaya a www.google.com y busque ahí. Si usted obtiene resultados diferentes, su computadora o su navegador pueden haber sido hackeados.
Si estos resultados son diferentes usted puede resetear su navegador de acuerdo a los tips anteiores para tratar de resolver este problema.

Tip #16
Agrande los resultados de su Búsqueda para facilitar la lectura.

Usted puede cambiar la resolución de la pantalla de manera que le permita ver y leer mejor los resultados de su búsqueda. Este proceso es básicamente el mismo en todos los navegadores y en todas las plataformas. A continuación presento algunos de los métodos más comunes para esto.

Para Chrome en Windows:

- Use la tecla **Ctrl**, para agrandar (**Ctrl+**), reducir (**Ctrl-**), y resetear (**Ctrl0**).
- Para un mouse con rueda, presione **Ctrl** y mueva el mouse hacia arriba o abajo.
- Menu (3 barras) **Zoom** (use + o – para cambiar).
- **F11** va a la pantalla completa, no olvide que con F11 regresa a lo normal.

Para IE en Windows (la mayoría de las versiones)
- Use la tecla **Ctrl**, para agrandar (**Ctrl+**), reducir (**Ctrl-**), y resetear (**Ctrl0**).
- Para un mouse con rueda, presione **Ctrl** y mueva hacia arriba o abajo.
- Menú (3 baras) **Zoom** (use + o – para cambiar).
- F11 va a pantalla completa, no olvide que con F11 regresa a lo normal.

Para Chrome en Mac:
- La tecla de commandos, Mac Command, (⌘), para agrandar (⌘ **+**), para recudir (⌘ **-**).
- El mouse de rueda no funciona para esto en una Mac.
- Menú – derecho arriba tres barras (hot dog).
- **Zoom** (use + o – para cambiar).

Tip #17
"Dónde" y "Cómo" busca afecta el resultado.

Hay mucho trabajo en la búsqueda por voz y Google Now. No todos estamos acostumbrados a hablarle a una computadora o teléfono, pero eso es el futuro. Google interpretará estos ítems de manera diferente, ya sea por los settings de la cuenta google que se esté utilizando, o debido a la historia de búsquedas en su computadora o navegador, si ya existiera alguna. Dónde se efectúa la búsqueda impacta, de manera ligera, sus resultados.

Para bien o para mal, Google desea conocerlo a usted para ayudarlo mejor y para dirigir su publicidad de manera más rentable.

Varios de los tips que siguen se aplican tanto para búsquedas tipeadas y búsquedas de voz y Google Now. Si usted busca en una computadora diferente con diferentes settings, los resultados serán de alguna manera direrentes. No se sorprenda si el gran trabajo de Google buscando resultados le brinda respuestas un poco diferentes dependiendo de dónde está usted realizando la búsqueda.

Además, si su navegador tiene un contenido o filtro familiar, los resultados pueden también ser difernetes.

Tip #18
"Cuándo" hace la búsqueda puede cambiar el resultado.

Con mucha frecuencia las cosas cambian rápidamente y Google asume que usted busca información actual (hot topics). Esto funciona a su favor en la mayoría de los casos. Pero si usted está tratando de encontrar algo un poco antiguo, necesita incluir más datos en su búsqueda, como el año o fechas. Presentaré más información al respecto más adelante.

Buscar precios de productos incluyendo vuelos aéreos e ítems más costosos, es más complicado. La mayoría de compañías que realizan ventas en línea, usan algoritmos complejos para determinar precios, y éstos pueden cambiar cada hora. Como la venta de entradas a bajo precio en teatros los Martes por la noche, porque se sabe que son funciones con poco público.

Usted no se está volviendo loco, los precios cambian muy a menudo.

Tip #19
Comience de manera simple y añada palabras según lo necesite.

Usted siempre debe iniciar su búsqueda con pocas palabras. Una vez que vea los resultados, tendrá una idea más clara de las palabras que debe añadir o que no deban ser consideradas (sí, usted puden eliminar palabras en su búsqueda). Las preguntas largas a veces le darán resultados inesperados.

Pasos de una búsueda:
- Comience con pocas palabras.
- Revise los resultados.
- Añada, retire, o excluya palabras (Tip 22) para afinar los resultados.
- Repita según lo necesite.

Tip #20
Probablemente usted no necesita usar comillas.

Google hace un gran trabajo buscando todas las palabras que usted ingresa, sin embargo, no está buscando las palabras o frases "exactas". Colocar las palabras entre comillas hará que Google busque las palabras que coincidan exactamente con las indicadas en la búsqueda. También puede usar wildcards (*) dentro de las citas, pero si las pone en el lugar incorrecto los resultados pueden ser peores. Use wildcards si tiene una idea exacta sobre dónde colocarlas.

Esto es cada vez menos importante dado que Google está mejorando sorprendentemente su interpretación de los que buscamos.

Tips sobre comillas de Google:
https://support.google.com/websearch/answer/136861?hl=en

Tip #21
Use un * (asterisco) para marcar sus Búsquedas (wildcards).

Usted puede usar un asterisco * como un wildcard para sus búsquedas. Esto funciona mejor si usted tiene las búsquedas con comillas. Repito, la Búsqueda de Google está mejorando tanto que este tip ya no es tan útil como solía serlo.

De todos modos, si usted combina comillas, wildcards y hace exclusiones (siguiente tip), tendrá una combinación poderosa.

Ejemplo de Wildcard directamente de Google:
" a * saved is a * earned"

Tip #22
Excluya una palabra en la Búsqueda.

Para hacer esto simplemente utilice el signo menos. A veces una palabra está asociada con más de un ítem, y usted quiere remover algunos de ellos.

Ejemplo de exclusión directamente de Google:
jaguar –car

Haga eso cuando busque información sobre el animal. Por supuesto esto no bloquea otra palabras relacionadas, como 'auto' por ejemplo. Esto nos lleva al prinicipio de comenzar sencillamente. Si usted encuentra resultados no deseados que tienen una palabra en común, excluya dicha palabra y los resultados que la contengan ya no se mostrarán.

Tips de Exclusión de Google (sí, en la misma página):
https://support.google.com/websearch/answer/136861?hl=en

Tip #23
Use la Búsqueda avanzada de Google.

Hay muchos tips, atajos, etc. para hacer búsquedas. A algunas personas les encanta y los han memorizado. Usted no tiene que recordarlos, sólo vaya a búsqueda Avanzada, que puede encontrarse haciendo click en Settings (boton derecho abajo, en la página principal de Google).

Si usted no ve Settings al pie de la página principal de Google, corra una búsqueda (cualquier cosa), haga click arriba a la derecha en la opción de la rueda y escoja Búsqueda Avanzada.

Opciones clave de Advance Search:
- Todos (All).
- Frase exacta (Exact phrase).
- No (para excluir palabras, None).
- Ultima actualización (Last Update).
- Búsqueda segura (Safe Search).
- Derecho de Uso (Usage rights).

Página web de Búsqueda Avanzada:
http://www.google.com/advanced_search

Ayuda para Búsqueda Avanzada:
https://support.google.com/websearch/answer/35890?hl=en

Tip #24
El resultado de su Búsqueda incluye herramientas de búsqueda, llamadas también pestañas (tabs).

Esto se vuelve un poco complicado (Ok, muy complicado). Google podría hacerlo mejor, por eso tengo que explicarlo, le doy a Google una calificación de C- por esto.

Cuando se ejecuta una búsqueda, generalmete por default es una búsqueda en la red, un **Web Search**, que usted puede afinar con comillas, wildcards, el signo menos, etc.

En sus resultados usted obtendrá algo parecido a esto en la parte superior de la página.

Web Shopping Images Videos Maps More Search Tools

Sin embargo, debido a algoritmos, reglas y a las mejores intentos de Google por proveer los mejores resultados posibles, tanto la lista de palabras que ingresó, el orden y las herramientas de búsqueda pueden cambiar. Usted podría obtener algo como lo siguiente:

Web Images News Videos Shopping More Search Tools

Dependiendo de lo que Google entiende que usted busca, le presentará opciones apropiadas para afinar los resultados. La mayoría de las opciones tiene sentido, algunas no. A pesar de que Google hace un trabajo fantástico encontrando información para usted, no siempre brinda opciones claras y consistentes para filtrar estos resultados. Un ejemplo de esto el la pestaña Hoteles, que usted no ve regularmente, pero si usted escoje Flights, la pestaña Hoteles aparecerá como una opción.

No voy a mencionar todas las opciones, pero la mayoría de ellas tiene un Filtro de tiempo, **Time Filter** que es probablemente el más útil. Además algunos resultados tienen la opción de ordenar la información de maneras como éstas:

- Por relevancia (Sorted by relevance) .
- Por fecha (Sorted by date).

El default, ordenar la información por Relevancia, funciona mejor.

El mejor consejo que le puedo dar es observar la variedad de opciones y decidir cuál lo acerca más a lo que usted busca. Algunos de los mejores filtros, incluyendo tiempo, los encuentra en

- **Search Tools**

Tip #25
Búsqueda de un tipo específico de documento (filetype).

Si usted está buscando documentos, no páginas web, y sabe qué tipo de documento está buscando, puede indicar la búsqueda de ese tipo de documentos solamente. Esto a menudo es muy útil si usted está buscando sets de datos a ser usados en análisis o gráficos.

Un ejemplo sería, filetype: pdf Primera Guerra Mundial, donde la extensión va a continuación de filetype (tipo de arhcivo), y se busca los documentos pdf sobre la Primera Guerra Mundial.

Ejemplos de búsqueda de tipos de documento:
- filetype:pdf World War 1.
- filetype:doc World War 1.

filetypes que Google comúnmente lista:
https://support.google.com/webmasters/answer/35287?hl=en

Tip #26
Use la Búsqueda para convertir casi cualquier cosa.

Google hará la conversión de casi cualquier medida. Tipee lo que desea convertir, asegurándose de que la conversión sea possible. No se puede convetir pintas a libras. En Estados Unidos las pintas son medidas de volumen, y las libras son medidas de peso. Cinco pintas de agua pesan menos que cinco libras de plomo.

Mientras trate de hacer conversiones de una misma unidad, como distancia, (millas a km,) etc., esto funcionará. Usted puede incluso escribir la pregunta, "Cuántas pulgadas hay en 37 millas", y obtendrá la respuesta. Este es el sorprendente poder de las búsquedas hoy en día, ingrese casi cualquier requerimiento y tendrá el resultado.

Usted puede también convertir algunas medidas científicas como temperatura, energía, fuerza, corriente eléctrica, etc. Algunas magníficas páginas y apps hacen un mejor trabajo para problemas más complejos, sin embargo usted puede comenzar con Google que es gratis y simple.

Ejemplos de conversión:

- 5 millas a km (obtendrá 8.04672).
- 5 US Dólares a Yen
- 2344320 pulgadas a millas

Tips de Conversiones y Matemáticas:
https://support.google.com/websearch/answer/3284611?hl=en

Tip #27
Use la Búsqueda para hacer matemáicas.

Google puede hacer matemáticas si usted solamente ingresa la formula. Un tip divertido al comienzo, fue usar mantemáticas para crear la forma de un corazón.

Cuando usted ingresa una formula en la búsquda, Google presentará la respuesta con su calculadora en línea. Es un buen trabajo e incluye varias funciones.

De cualquier modo, como el tip de conversión anterior, existen muchos apps sobresalientes de matemáticas para teléfonos y tabletas hoy en día. Imagino que mucha gente los usa. Hay una gran diferencia entre el resutado visual en una página web y el de un app telefónico. El app es más fácil de usar y leer. Una característica\tip que está dejando de ser utilizada, pero está siendo reemplazada por algo mejor.

Funciones Matemáticas disponibles:
- Matemátca Básica.
- Funciones como seno, coseno, tangente (sen, cos, tan).
- Esquemas, incluyendo gráficos 3D (dependiendo de su navegador).

Tips en Conversión y Matemáticas (igual que el anterior):
https://support.google.com/websearch/answer/3284611?hl=en

Tip #28
Busque datos públicos y visualice los

resultados.

Google tiene sets públicos de datos que pueden ser accesados. Usted puede encontrar esta información por usted mismo de la fuente original, pero tal vez no sea tan fácil de buscar y utilizar. También es conveniente tener varios sets de datos en una sola ubicación.

Google tiene una buena herramienta de gráficos que le permite visualizar su información. Puede usted además compartir su gráfico con un link. Desafortunadamente en la actualidad Google no le permite exportar los datos, sólo un link a la fuente de información, lo cual debe permitir algún método de descarga.

Algunos sets de datos están obsoletos (dos o tres años de anterioridad), por lo que debe revisar las fechas antes de comenzar.

Características de Datos Públicos:
- Abundantes sets de datos de varias fuentes.
- Buena capacidad de gráficos.
- Habilidad para crear cuadros y links a ellos.
- No exportación de datos.
- Algunos datos son un poco antiguos.

Tip #29
Busque el estatus de vuelos aéreos.

Google compró una compañía de software de vuelos (ITA) hace pocos años para tener acceso directo a información de vuelos. No pueden vender pasajes porque la gente usa Google para buscar precios y Google tendría un ventaja injusta.

Ejemplo de búsqueda de Vuelos (carrier y número de vuelo):
- Southwest 234

Información de vuelos desde Google (la mayoría de carriers):
- https://www.google.com/flights

Flightstats hace un buen trabajo de seguimiento también (no es un

producto Google):
- http://www.flightstats.com/go/Home/home.do

Tip #30
Busque el estatus del envío de un paquete (UPS, USPS, FedEx, etc.)

Google puede infromar el estatus de envíos en tiempo real (UPS, USPS, FedEx). Todo lo que usted tiene que hacer es ingresar el código del paquete enviado y aparecerá toda la información. UPS, FedEx, y otros tienen formatos de más de un número. Usualmente el código de seguimiento del paquete es suficiente. En caso tenga dificultades añada un prefijo tal como FedEx antes del código para obtener el resultado esperado. (FedEx tiene 12 or 15 dígitos generalmete).

Ejemplo de Búsqueda de estado de envios;
- 345676545675
- FedEx 345676545675.

Tip #31
Busque la cartelera y el horario de las funciones.

Me encantan Fandango, y sitios web y apps que muestran avances de películas y horario de funciones. Algunas veces uno se cansa de las propagandas de películas y comerciales que aparecen de repente y "sólo quiere ver el horario de la cartelera." Basta buscar con la palabra **movies** y usted verá la cartelera local. Haga click en la película que escoja y obtendrá el horaio local de las funciones.

Fandango parece tener un poquito más de precisión. Aunque en raras ocaciones, he encontrado los horarios de Google atrasados en un día. A menudo las salas de cine cambian películas y horarios de acuerdo a la demanda. Además usted puede comprar tickets en la gran mayoría de los casos.

Tal vez algún empleado inteligente de Google pueda escribir una pequeña comparación entre sus horarios y los de otros para señalar y resolver discrepancias.

Para buscar el horario de cartelera:
- Busque la palabra **movie**.
- Haga click en la película que desee para encontrar el horario de las funciones.

Peículas por sala de cine (simple y grandioso):
http://www.google.com/movies

Usted puede encontrar cosas sorprendentes, los viajes en el tiempo existen, películas a $1:
http://www.starplexcinemas.com/locations.php?theaterid=3002

Tip #32
Encuentre pronósticos del clima.

En estos días hay más apps para pronósticos del clima que los que puede usted contar. Google tiene el suyo, simple y claro. Si usted quiere "un pronóstico simple", éste es el sitio que debe consultar.

Ejemplos:
- Tipee **forecast** seguido de la ciudad y el estado, o el código postal. (ZIP code).
- Forecast Concord, CA.
- Forecast 94521.

US National Weather Service es una alternativa:
http://www.weather.gov/

Tip #33
Busque valores en el Mercado Bursátil.

Usted puede encontrar valores del Mercado tan sólo utilizando el símbolo de stock. Hay muchos apps incluyendo el de Google,

Finance, que le permiten hacer seguimiento a las cotizaciones, pero si usted sólo necesita una vista rápida, esto será suficiente.

Para buscar el precio de un stock:

- Ingrese el símbolo del stock y usted verá su precio. Por ejemplo, csco para Cisco.
- Si el símbolo del stock es el mismo que el nombre de la compañía, como IBM, usted obtendrá links al lado izquierdo, pero el precio del stock se verá a la derecha. Haga click en el precio del stock y obtendrá el cuadro de información.

Información del Mercado de Valores en Google:
https://www.google.com/finance

Sitios de Stock market de otras fuentes (Google no es el mejor en todo):
- http://finance.yahoo.com/market-overview/
- http://markets.wsj.com/usoverview?mod=WSJ_hpp_marketdata
- http://www.bloomberg.com/markets/
- http://investing.money.msn.com/investments/market-summary/

Tip #34
Busque una localidad por ciudad o código postal (ZIP code).

Usted puede indicar que la búsqueda sea sólo local, añadiendo el nombre de la ciudad o el código postal al final de lo que está buscando. Mucha gente usa aplicaciones de mapas para buscar localmente, lo cual es más fácil y permite ver lo buscado en el mapa. La tendencia actual de usar Google Now con tarjetas irá en aumento. Una tarjeta de Google es un resumen breve de información útil, basada usualmente en la hora del día y en su ubicación. Piense en tráfico, citas, clima o resutados de competencias.

Además, si usted ha entrado a Google, éste usualmente conoce su ubicación por default, de manera que este tip es más usado para otras localizaciones. Si está planeando un viaje y quiere encontrar un local en su destino, por ejemplo la mejor pizza en New York,

- Pizza New York
- Pizza 10001.

Tip #35
Busque Patentes usando Google Patent Search.

Google tiene una gran fuente de referencia de patentes que es divertida y educativa para todos, que usted encontrará más fácil de usar que el sitio del gobierno, el cual incluyo también.

Búsqueda de Google Patent:
 https://www.google.com/?tbm=pts&gws_rd=ssl

Búsqueda Avanzada Google de Patentes :
 http://www.google.com/advanced_patent_search

Sobre Google Patent Search:
 https://support.google.com/faqs/answer/2539193?hl=en&ref_topic=3368954

Sitio de referencia sobre Búsqueda de Patentes del gobierno US:
 http://www.uspto.gov/patents/process/search/index.jsp

Tip #36
Cree un perfil de estudiante en Google Académico.

Google tiene una búsqueda específica para los estudiantes, que contiene grandes aplicaciones como la Búsqueda de Patentes (tip #35), lo cual lo hace fantástico. Le sugiero establecer un perfil académico para guardar todas sus referencias, lo cual toma un minuto.

http://scholar.google.com/intl/en/scholar/citations.html.

Alcances clave de Google Scholar:
- Muy buenas búsquedas incluyendo patentes y casos legales.
- Puede guardar sus búsquedas\artículos.
- Brinda el formato apropiado de las citas (los 3 formatos principales).
- Formato apropiado de citas (**Repetido & Excelente**).
- Citación por números y artículos relacionados.
- Links a bibliotecas, a subscripciones en su escuela\biblioteca. Es un poco técnico pero un gran logro para estudiantes de college. La biblioteca y el departamento técnico de la escuela pueden ayudarle.

Búsqueda de Google Scholar:
http://scholar.google.com/

Tips sobre búsqueda de Google Scholar:
http://scholar.google.com/intl/en-US/scholar/help.html

Un ejemplo de búsqueda en Google Académico con Cite

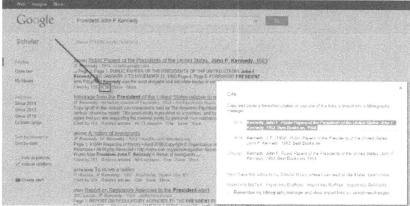

Tip #37
Use la herramienta de investigación Google Docs.

Hay una gran manera de colocar en un documento Google la

información encontrada, y añadir a esto una cita correcta automáticamente. Haga esto y su profesor estará contento. Google Docs no cubre tanto como Google Académico pero tiene varias de las mismas aplicaciones.

Lo que hace es crear un panel lateral a su derecha con las búsquedas y resultados. Es muy fácil crear un documento.

Beneficios de Google Docs:
- Con el panel lateral puede ver su trabajo fácilmente.
- Trabaja con Google docs, no con hojas de cálculo o slides.
- Sobrevuela otros links primero para Preview, Insert Link, o Cite.
- Si cita los resultados, Google añade al documento las citas en formato correcto automáticamente.

Ayuda de Google Docs Research
- https://support.google.com/docs/answer/2481802?hl=en

Tip #38
Revisión de Citas, porque es importante.

El tema de las citas es muy importante, por eso añado este recurso adicional. La mayoría de los niños debe estar utilizando uno o más de estos tips, y seguramente tanto ellos como los profesores tienen sus preferencias. Mis hijos usan easybib, que parece ser el más popular.

Si usted es padre de un estudiante no familiarizado con estas aplicaciones tome unos minutos para revisar algunas de ellas. Una cita en formato inapropiado no debe ser el motivo por el cual su estudiante reciba una calificación baja.

Recursos de Citatión alternativos:
- http://www.easybib.com/
- http://www.mendeley.com/
- http://www.bibme.org/

Tip #39
Encuentre y lea libros de dominio público.

Google tiene una búsqueda específica sólo para libros, muchos de los cuales usted puede leer de manera gratuita. Usted puede enlazar su perfil de Google con Google Books para crear una biblioteca personal. Google aún está muy lejos de trabajar como una cuenta unificada. Estos son los links y setups que se requieren.

El link a Project Gutenberg no está relacionado con Google pero es otra gran referencia para búsqueda de libros.

Búsqueda en Google Book:
http://books.google.com/

Ayuda de Google Book:
https://support.google.com/books/?hl=en#topic=4359341

Búsqueda en Project Gutenberg:
http://www.gutenberg.org/

Tip #40
Personalice su Buscador Google.

Sí, es impresionate y excelente. Esta es una de las características de Google más subutilizadas. Es usada mayormente por profesores, y tiene una gran variedad de usos.

No sólo puede usar el poder de Google Search y personalizarlo, usted puede también compartirlo con el mundo, publicarlo en su página web y mucho más.

Para personalizar su búsqueda (necesitar haber accesado a Google):
1. https://www.google.com/cse/all.
2. Haga click en **New Search Engine** (arriba, izquierda).

3. Añada páginas o sitios de internet que desee incluir.
4. Asígnele un nombre (como quiera usted llamarlo).
5. Haga click en **Create** (al pie).

Ahora puede añadirlo a su sitio Web o hacerlo un URL público que puede compartir o ser enlazado como un link por otras personas.

Información de Google custom search:
https://support.google.com/customsearch/?hl=en#topic=4513742

No puedo imaginar porqué no se usa en todos los colegios. Por ejemplo, si usted es profesor de historia y tiene 30 sitios de referencia sobre Historia de América, puede hacerlos disponibles para sus estudiantes en 10 minutos.
Si usted es muy fanático de los fósiles, hasta dirige reuniones los Jueves en el museo local, usted puede setear su propia búsqueda cubriendo los mejores 20 sitios de internet con este tópico.

Si usted administra una escuela elementaria o enseña a sus hijos en casa, esto sirve para garantizar la seguridad de sus búsquedas. Sólo note que considero que usted puede cubrir toda la información que necesita con 30 o 40 sitios web. Esto es genial para niños pequeños pero no funciona para jóvenes que necesitan un área de investigación más amplia.

Si alguno quisiera compilar 1,500 sitios educativos que cubran el 95% de las necesidades de los estudiantes, sería estupendo. Nuestros hijos podrían realizar las búsquedas sin nosotros temer que algo inapropiado aparezca. Hey, yo creo que se puede hacer un gran trabajo con sólo 500 sitios.

Tip #41
Use Alertas de Google.

El Buscador es bueno, pero qué tal si existiera una manera fácil de hacer que Google le envíe lo que usted está buscando? En un tiempo existía Google Reader el cual era un lector RSS. Los lectores RSS aún existen pero no llegaron a ser tan populares como se pensó.

Google aún tiene el Alerta Google, una búsqueda que le envía un correo electrónico cada vez que un nuevo ítem es hallado. Digamos que su compañía trabaja con baterías de Litio. Usted puede ordenar a Google que le envíe alertas con las últimas noticias sobre este tema para mantenerlo a usted actualizado.

Para setear Google Alerts:
1. Vaya a esta página:
2. https://www.google.com/alerts?hl=en&tab=33.
3. Tipee una palabra o frase.
4. Haga click en **Create Alert** (las opciones default usualmente trabajan mejor).
5. Si usted no ha registrado su acceso, se le requerirá acceder.
6. Su cuenta de correo electrónico comenzará a recibir alertas diarias (ése es el default).

Información adicional:
- Usted puede setear cuantas alertas desee. Algunas personas crean una cuenta de correo Gmail especialmente para recibir las alertas y las revisan regularmente por ejemplo, al inicio de cada semana.
- Una gran ventaja de las alertas es que usted tienen la información ordenada por fecha y puede reconocer la primera información y los seguimientos.
-

Información sobre Google Alerts:
https://support.google.com/alerts/?hl=en

Tip #42
Reservado, es la respuesta para todo.

Si está usted interesado, chequéelo. Fue también el primer número del gigante Googleplex.

Tip #43
Busque y navegue de manaera anónima (es un tip largo porque es complicado).

Usted puede borrar la historia de sus búsquedas y de su navegación. También puede apagar el registro de historia en casi todos los casos, de manera que siempre esté apagado. Chrome no tiene una manera fácil de hacerlo.

Recuerde que sólo voy a cubrir búsquedas en Google e historia de la navegación. No cubro todos los rincones desde donde usted está siendo rastreado.

Usted está siendo rastreado por:
- Su proveedor de búsquedas (Google, Bing, Yahoo).
- Su Navegador
- Su proveedor de Internet (Comcast, AT&T etc.).
- Su proveedor de línea telefónica.
- Los sitios de Internet (Websites) que visita.
- Su proveedor de correo electrónico (Google, Yahoo, Microsoft, Apple) puede leer sus correos, pues ellos se reservan el derecho de hacerlo.
- Su empleador rastrea lo que usted hace en sus sistemas, o cualquier Sistema autorizado para conectarse a su red.
- Los lugares públicos como escuelas y bibliotecas utilizan software de rastreo por seguridad.
- Cualquier vecino si usted no tiene clave para su red inalámbrica WiFi.
- Redes Sociales (Facebook, etc.).
- Apps, especialmente los que tienen aplicaciones en línea.
- Asumo que el gobierno rastrea probablemente todo.
- Como fan de los Expedientes X, le aseguro que también los aliens.

Veamos lo mundano, cómo borrar la historia de búsquedas y navegación.

Borrar Historia de Búsquedas

Las búsquedas en Google van a seguir registrándose a menos que apague Historia de Búsquedas (muy fácil). Usted puede borrar sus búsquedas más recientes, pero la mayoría prefiere borrar toda la historia completea. Asumiento que Google está funcionando sincronizadamente, esto funciona en todos sus dispositivos sin necesidad de hacerlo en cada uno de ellos.

Deletear la Historia de Google **(Chrome IE Win\Mac\Android\iPhone):**
1. https://history.google.com/history/.
2. Settings gear (derecha, arriba).
3. Escoja **Settings**.
4. Vaya a la pestaña Cuenta de Historia **Account History** tab.
5. Algunas veces tiene que hacer click en Account History dos veces para ver todo. Si usted ve sólo Búsqueda no está viendo todo.
6. Hay varias áreas que puede chequear con **Manage History.**
7. La mayoría de las áreas incluyendo **Things you search for** le permiten seleccionar y luego borrar.
8. Para **Places you've been** (Google maps etc.) se borra en el lado izquierdo.

Apagar la Historia de Búsquedas

Para apagar el registro en la Historia de Búsquedas en Google **(Chrome IE Win\MAC\Androide\iPhone):**
1. En la pestaña Account History de arriba.
2. Haga click otra vez para asegurarse de que todos los ítems se muestren.
3. Hay un botón **Pause** en cada área.
4. Haga click en ese botón y luego haga click en **Pause History** para confirmar.

Tips de Google para apagar o borrar la historia de búsquedas:
• https://support.google.com/websearch/answer/465?hl=en

Borre la Historia del Navegador

Borrar la historia de su navegador en Chrome supone borrarla en todos sus dispositivos en los que usted está accediendo. De cualquier modo, he encontrado que esto no funciona siempre. De modo que recomiendo hacerlo en cada dispositivo por seguridad.

Para borrar la historia del navegador **(Chrome for Win\Mac)**:

1. Menú Chrome (tres barras, ariiba, derecha), llamado también hotdog.
2. **History**.
3. Si usted accesa a más de un dispositivo (teléfono, tableta, etc.) usted debe ver la historia en esos dispositivos también.
4. Haga click en el botón **Clear Browsing Data**.
5. Escoja **from the beginning of time** en el menú de cascada.
6. Generalmente usted desea marcar como chequeado lo siguiente
7. **Browsing History, Download History, Cookies, Cached images.**
8. Chequear Cookies afectará su verificación de dos pasos si es que la está utilizando. Usted sólo tiene que marcar con un check remember this device again, la próxima vez que se conecte.
9. Haga click en el botón **Clear Browsing** al pie.

Informacón adicional:
- Puede tomar dos o tres minutos limpiar la historia.
- Usted podría notar que Chrome funciona más rápido (esto es bueno).

Tips Google sobre seteo de privacidad **(Chrome)**:
https://support.google.com/chrome/answer/114836?hl=en

Para borrar la historia del navegador **(IE para Windows)**:

1. Asumiendo que usted tiene visible el menú (siempre una buena idea).
2. **Tools**.
3. **Delete Browser History**.
4. Generalmente debe marcar con un check lo siguiente.
5. **Preserve Favorites, Temporary Internet files, Cookies,**

History, Download History.
6. **Delete** (los defaults chequeados están bien).

Microsoft recibe una A por ser tan fácil usarlo.

Tips para la Historia del Navegador de Microsoft **(IE)**:
- http://windows.microsoft.com/en-us/internet-explorer/manage-delete-browsing-history-internet-explorer#ie=ie-11

Para borrar la historia del navegador **(Chrome para teléfonos Androides)**:
1. Botón **Menú**.
2. **Settings**.
3. **Privacy**.
4. **Clear Browsing data** (al pie).
5. Generalmente debe marcar con un check los siguientes ítems.
6. **Clear browsing history, Clear the cache, Clear Cookies**
7. Haga click en **Clear** para confirmar.
8. Presione la tecla Back dos veces para regresar a la web.

Para borrar la historia del navegador **(Chrome para iPhone)**:
1. Menú de tres barras (también llamado Hot Dog).
2. History.
3. Aclare Browsing History.
4. Haga click en **Clear Browsing Data** (al pie).
5. **Clear Browsing History**
6. **Clear Browsing History** (con el basurero para confirmar)

Apagar la Historia del Navegador

Para apagar la historia del navegador **(Chrome para Windows <u>no es sencillo</u>)**:
1. Añada una pestaña de modo Incógnito. Debe hacer ésto cada vez, no es automático.
2. Menú Chrome (tres barras, arriba, derecha), llamado también hotdog.
3. **New Incognito window**.
O la manera complicada, y si usted comete un error Chrome podría

no funcionar.

1. Primero copie el ítem o atajo que usó para iniciar Chrome y pegue una segunda versión (en caso de que cometa un error).
2. Edite las propiedades en el archivo de la aplicación o atajo, añadiendo –incógnito al final (un poco complicado, pasos a continuación).
3. Haga click derecho en las propiedades del ícono de la aplicación para Chrome.
4. Bajo Target, vaya al final y añada un espacio y luego añada – incognito y grábelo, sálvelo.
5. Debe verse algo como esto:
6. "C:\Program Files (x86)\Google\Chrome\Application\chrome.exe" – incognito

7. Cada vez que inicie Chrome desde este ícono, estará en modo incógnito (el hombre con el sombrero siempre se mostrará).

Para apagar la historia del navegador **(IE para Windows en la mayoría de las versiones):**
1. Asumiendo que usted tiene el menú visible (siempre una buena idea), **Tools**.
2. **Internet Options**.
3. Pestaña **General**.
4. Bajo **Browsers History**.
5. Haga click en **Settings.**
6. Pestaña **History**.
7. **Days to keep pages in History** setear a 0.
8. OK.
9. OK.

Microsoft obtiene otra A por ser esto tan fácil.

Apagar la historia del navegador **(Chrome para Mac):**
- No hay manera fácil de hacer esto en una Mac. Si alguien sabe una buena manera de hacerlo (debe ser simple), hágamelo saber.
- Fijando el archivo de Historia bajo Library/Application Support/Google/Chrome/Default puede no ser una buena idea. Puede causar problemas con actualizaciones o dañar Chrome de alguna manera inesperada.

Apagar la historia del navegador (**Chrome para Androide y Chrome para iPhone):**
- La única manera fácil de hacer esto es usar el modo Incógnito.
- Si alguien conoce alguna manera más fácil (no hacks) hágamelo saber.

Tip #44
Vea mapas de museos.

Google ha hecho mapas de museos y visitarlos es como un paseo remoto. Si usted está estudiando e investigando sobre museos, vale la pena probarlo.

Hablando de paseos, hay un gran app de Google con el nombre Field Trips. La próxima vez que se encuentre viajando, revíselo. En años recientes se han añadido sitios importantes no históricos y referencias, y es todavía un gran app.

Museums maps:
https://www.google.com/maps/views/streetview/art-project?gl=us

Tip #45
Use maps y Google Earth.

Si usted está buscando un lugar, no existe mejor opción que encontrarlo con Google Maps. Le brinda un gran sentido de ubicación y ambiente. Muchas veces la búsqueda se hace mejor en maps. A veces una búsqueda abre los mapas porque Google decide que de esa manera el resultado será mejor (y esto es correcto a menudo.

Si usted busca un restaurante, tipee la palabra 'restaurante' en mapas y se resaltarán todos los restaurantes cercanos a usted. De igual maera para zapaterías, etc. Mapas por sí mismo puede cubrir un set independiente de tips. Los siguientes son mis tips favoritos. Excepto por los dos últimos sobre enviar una ubicación, todos funcionan de igual manera en todos los dispositivos.

Tips para búsquedas en Google Maps:
- Zooming in le dará detalles de tiendas y negocios.
- Un dato general, le dará todos los resultados, mientras que un nombre en particular, por ejemplo, Starbucks, le mostrará todos los locales cercanos.
- Si usted hace click en un local, un teatro por ejemplo, a menudo le brindará los eventos al pie del resultado. Haga click en uno de ellos y le mostrará aún más eventos.
- Usted puede buscar horarios de transporte público que son de mucha ayuda. Haga click en Transit (se ve como un bus), ingrese su destino, y se mostrará los horarios disponibles.
- Si usted desea compartir una dirección o localidad, presione en la localidad hasta que el pin se muestre. La dirección se mostrará debajo del mapa, baje un poco y podrá compartir la localidad. (sólo funciona en teléfonos y tabletas). Un buen ejemplo es ven por mí a este lugar. Si usted lo envía como un texto, la persona que lo recibe puede hacer click en él y se abrirá Mapas con las indicaciones para llegar.
- Aunque me agrada la capacidad de enviar ubicaciones de Mapas de Google, mi hijo aún prefiere el GPS Share Androide por Ken Kinder por que es un poco más simple.

Tips sobre Maps de Google (note que los tips para teléfonos móviles están al pie:
https://support.google.com/maps/?hl=en#topic=3092425

Tip #46
Cuándo <u>no</u> usar Mapas y Google Earth.

A pesar de su gran utilidad no trate de usar las aplicaciones de mapas geográficos de su teléfono cuando se encuentre acampando o fuera de la ciudad. Este funciona de manera diferente a un GPS, necesita conectarse a la red de su teléfono. Aunque usted puede descargar parte de Google Maps u otro app de GPS, no es algo confiable.

Por ejemplo, si usted va a escalar montañas, y quiere añadir seguridad a su GPS, compre un dispositivo GPS autónomo. De preferencia uno que use baterías estándares reemplazables.

Tip #47
Busque Imágenes.

Cuando desee encontrar una imagen o un cuadro, como un pintura famosa, Google le ayuda de diferentes maneras. Una es utilizando una extensión para Chrome. No soy fanático de extensions y la tendencia es dejarlas de lado, aunque hay algunas muy buenas.

Aunque Google hace un gran trabajo revisando métodos de búsqueda de imágenes, generalmente copio el URL de la imagen. Si está usted usando Chrome todo lo que tiene que hacer es darle click derecho en la imagen y seleccionar Search Google para esta imagen.

Para usar Chrome para buscar una imagen:
1. Haga click derecho en la imagen.
2. Elija **Search Google for this image**.

Para usar búsqueda de imágenes de Chrome copie el método URL:
1. Haga click derecho en la imagen.
2. **Copy Image URL**.
3. Vaya a este sitio de internet
4. http://images.google.com/.
5. Péguelo en la caja de búsquedas.
6. Para mejorar la exactitud haga click en **Search by Image** (arriba, izquierda).

Tip de Google para búsquedas de imagen
http://www.google.com/insidesearch/features/images/searchbyimage.html

Alternativa para búsqueda de Imágenes (TinEye):
https://www.tineye.com/

Tip #48
Busque con su cámara.

Dije que la Búsqueda está cambiando. Un teléfono inteligente (Smartphone) tiene opciones de búsqueda tomando una foto. Existe un app de Inmuebles que le dará el precio de una casa tan sólo tomando una foto de ella. Hay demasiados apps para listarlos todos, útiles para hacer scans, buscar o traducir con su cámara, por eso visite la tienda de apps (app store).

Inicialmente, algunos de los apps de búsqueda más populares eran lectores de códigos de barra, escáners. Usted podía simplemente entrar en línea o ir a una tienda y leer un código de barras y encontrar información detallada incluyendo precios. Usted aún puede hacer esto, pero muchas compañías utilizan sus propios códigos de barra sólo para sus tiendas. Esto disminuyó la utilidad de estos apps, pero son gratis y toma un minuto usarlos.

Si usted está usando Google Now (más tips más adelante), éste tiene una opción para buscar con la cámara. Google Goggles (Android).

Para usar la búsqueda con Cámara de Google Now:
1. Menú Camera.
2. **Settings**.
3. Toque **Search from Camera**.
4. Marque con un check la caja **Search from Camera**.

Información sobre la opción de búsqueda con Cámara de Google:
https://support.google.com/websearch/answer/186334?hl=en

Tip #49
Encuentre algunos buenos apps para teléfonos (Google no puede con todo).

Hoy en día el buscador Google es casi mágico Aún así, no puede competir con apps de uso específico. Hey, vivo en California y uso con gusto el app de alerta de terremotos, Earthquake Alert!, por Josh Clemm (sólo para Androides). No he encontrado ningún otro que se le parezca. Si usted busca informacón médica WebMD es un gran app que le brinda mucha y muy buena información con rapidez.

Tengo un Galaxy Androide y un iPhone, con más apps instalados que los que quiero admitir (la mayoría en el Galaxy). Trato de no sobrepasar los 500 pero superé los 1200 en el Galaxy antes de depurarlos.

Visitar la tienda de apps de vez en cuando le ayudará a encontrar uno que deje avergozado a Google en un área específica de búsqueda. Ningún proveedor de búsquedas puede ser el mejor en todo.

Esta es una lista rápida de algunos de los mejores apps, algunos sólo para Androide. Estoy omitiendo los obvios como Facebook. Lo siento, soy friki. Mi consejo es que si usted cuenta con poco tiempo (como casi todos), busque un app inspiracional que haga su día mejor. Los primeros dos de la lista son para eso, cuando tenga más tiempo explore el resto.

Otra nota en Seguridad. La tienda Apple es segura y las aplicaciones han sido cuidadosamente examinadas. Lo mismo es cierto para la tienda Google Play. De cualquier modo, existen otros lugares donde usted puede obtener apps para Androides. No recomiendo obtener apps para Androides de otro lugar que no sea Google Play, la tienda de apps de Amazon o la tienda de apps de Samsung, si usted tiene un teléfono Samsung.

50 apps interesantes y extraordinarios para Androide (muchos también para iPhone):
Inspirational Quotes Free (por Vankiros), Motivational Quote for Success (por Piapps), Twilight (el app no la película, para deshacerse de la luz azul y cormir mejor), TED, Fireworks, Talking Tom, Magic Fluids, KidsDoodle (es bueno tener apps divertidos para niños, pueden salvar nuestro día), Google Sky Maps, Moon 3D, 3D UFO (seamos paranoides), Google Field Trip, GPS Share, Spotify, projectM (muy Buenos efectos de pantalla basados en la música ejecutada), IMDb, Netflix, Share Apps (por Squid Tooth) Pandora, Fandango, iFunny (tenga cuidado, puede ser una pérdida de tiempo), Digg, Meetup, Kindle Reader, Zing (Vea quién está en su red y más), Earth Quake Alert (por Josh), Red Cross First Aid (hay muchos apps de la Cruz Roja), WebMD, Google Hangouts, Hangouts Dialer,

Speed Test (by OOKLA), Quick Pic, Remote Desktop, Google Keep (muy bueno para tomar notas y hacer listas de tareas), Zillow, Paper Camera, Gas Buddy, Mint, Google Drive, Disk Usage (por Ivan Volosyuk, muy buena manera de ver el espacio en su Androide), ES File Explorer, List my apps, AIO Toolbox, Antutu, Google Photos, Network Signal Info, Barcode Scanner (por ZXing Team), BART Usher (para el área de San Francisco), Google Device Manager, Torque (también necesita un adaptador Bluetooth de $15 - $40 para leer códigos de autos).

Tip #50
Comandos Google Now (también llamados Google Search App – sí, es confuso).

Como dije al principio la barra de búsqueda se está convirtiendo también en barra de comandos. Le daré a conocer algunos de los commandos por voz de Google Now. Todos los comados de búsqueda comienzan con "Busca", éste es un commando de Google Now que ayuda a entender lo que usted está tratando de buscar.

Estos commandos comienzan a integrarse con apps volviendose más potentes pero también potencialmente confusos. Puede haber pequeñas diferencias en su uso entre Androides, iPhones, Chrome OS, y Chrome Browser en computadoras Windows o Mac.

Ejemplos de Comandos Google Now:
- **Busca** (lo que desse buscar en Google).
- **Recuérdame** (acción, ej. comprar leche) en (cantidad de horas).
- **Establece la alarma para las** (hora).
- **Annadir Nota** (Posts to Keep, Evernote y otros apps).
- **LLamar a** (contacto).
- **LLévame a** (lugar, usa mapas).
- **Ir a / Abrir** (página de internet).
- **What's this song** (Funciona como Shazam).

Página principal de soporte de Google Now:
https://support.google.com/websearch/topic/4409793?rd=1

Revisión breve de Google Now:
https://support.google.com/websearch/answer/2819496?hl=en&ref_topic=6032673

Extra Tip
Un tip extra, sólo para divertirnos (si usted es muy bueno en búsquedas y le piden ayuda).

Comenzamos y terminamos con un poco de diversión. Cuando le hagan una pregunta sencilla, que puede ser consultada fácilmente en Google, utilice el sitio **Let Me Google That For You** con una simple dirección, LMGTFY.COM.

Tipee la pregunta en dicho sitio y encontrará un link. Usted puede enviar este link, que busca la pregunta en Google y provee las respuestas. Pruébelo y demostrará que usted realmente sabe efectuar búsquedas, aún con un truco sofisticado. Note que este sitio de internet no es parte de Google.

Dígame qué opina.

Espero que usted haya aprendido nuevos tips. Por favor, hágame saber sus favoritos o si olvidé alguno. Espero actualizar estos tips el 2015 e incluiré todas las respuestas que pueda.

Gracias.
Tom

Feeback50Searchtips@gmail.com

www.ingramcontent.com/pod-product-compliance
Lightning Source LLC
Chambersburg PA
CBHW071006050326
40689CB00014B/3513